THE

TEACHER'S ASSISTANT;

OR,

A SYSTEM OF PRACTICAL ARITHMETIC:

WHEREIN

THE SEVERAL RULES OF THAT USEFUL SCIENCE ARE ILLUSTRATED BY A VARIETY OF EXAMPLES,

A LARGE PROPORTION OF WHICH ARE IN

FEDERAL MONEY.

THE WHOLE DESIGNED

TO ABRIDGE THE LABOUR OF TEACHERS, AND TO FACILITATE THE INSTRUCTION OF YOUTH.

A NEW EDITION, WITH CORRECTIONS AND ADDITIONS BY THE AUTHOR.

REVISED.

COMPILED BY STEPHEN PIKE.

PHILADELPHIA:
PUBLISHED BY M. POLOCK,
No. 6 COMMERCE STREET.

EXPLANATION OF CHARACTERS.

Signs.	*Significations.*
=	equal ; as 20s. = *L.* 1.
+	more ; as 6+2=8.
−	less ; as 8−2=6.
×	into, with, or multiplied by ; as, 6×2=12.
÷	by (*i. e.* divided by) as, 6÷2=3 ; or, 2)6(3.
: :: :	proportionality ; as, 2 : 4 :: 6 : 12.
$\sqrt{}$ or $\sqrt[2]{}$	Square Root ; as, $\sqrt[2]{64}=8$.
$\sqrt[3]{}$	Cube Root ; as, $\sqrt[3]{64}=4$.
$\sqrt[4]{}$	Fourth Root ; as, $\sqrt[4]{16}=2$, &c.
———	A Vinculum ; denoting the several quantities over which it is drawn, to be considered jointly as a simple quantity

CONTENTS.

	PAGE
Numeration	5
Simple Addition	8
Simple Subtraction	10
Simple Multiplication	11
Simple Division	15
Federal Money	20
Simple Reduction	28
Compound Addition	40
Compound Subtraction	47
Compound Multiplication	53
Compound Division	57
Compound Reduction	64
The Single Rule of Three	70
The Double Rule of Three	78
Practice	82
Tare and Tret	93
Simple Interest	97
Insurance, Commission, and Brokerage	107
Compound Interest	109
Discount	110
Equation	112
Barter	113
Loss and Gain	115
Fellowship	117
Exchange	120
Vulgar Fractions	127
Decimal Fractions	142

PAGE
Involution 153
Square Root 155
Cube Root 158
A general Rule for extracting the Roots of all Powers 160
Alligation 161
Position 166
Arithmetical Progression 169
Geometrical Progression 172
Compound Interest by Decimals 175
Discount at Compound Interest 177
Annuities at Compound Interest 179
Annuities in Reversion 183
Perpetuities 184
Permutation 185
Combination 186
Duodecimals 186
Promiscuous Questions 190

ARITHMETIC.

Arithmetic is the art of computing by numbers. It has five principal rules for its operations; viz. numeration, addition, subtraction, multiplication, and division.

NUMERATION.

Numeration teaches to write or express numbers by figures, and to read numbers thus written or expressed.

In treating of numbers, the following terms are employed: viz. *unit*, *ten*, *hundred*, *thousand*, and *million;* as also *billion*, *trillion*, and some others. But the latter are seldom used.

A unit is a single one.
A ten is ten units.
A hundred is ten tens.
A thousand is ten hundreds.
A million is ten hundred thousands.

Note.—As it takes ten hundred thousands to make a million, when we express a number greater than a thousand, and less than a million, we use *tens of thousands*, or *hundreds of thousands*, or both, as the case requires. Likewise, to express a number greater than a million, we employ *tens of millions*, or *hundreds of millions*, &c.

The following are the figures used in numeration, with their names above them.

One	two	three	four	five	six	seven	eight	nine
1	2	3	4	5	6	7	8	9

Each of these figures represents the number which its name denotes; but it is understood to be that number of units, or that number of tens, or that number of hundreds, &c., according to its relative place: which is exemplified in the following tables:

TABLE FIRST.

Hundred million	Ten million	Million	Hundred thousand	Ten thousand	Thousand	Hundred	Ten	Unit
1	1	1,	1	1	1,	1	1	1

TABLE SECOND

Hundreds of millions	Tens of millions	Millions	Hundreds of thousands	Tens of thousands	Thousands	Hundreds	Tens	Units
2	2	2,	2	2	2,	2	2	2

These tables show that in using figures to express numbers, they are placed in a horizontal row—the first figure at the right hand representing one or more units, the next tens, the next hundreds, &c. Thus a 1 is *one unit*, or *one ten*, or *one hundred*, &c., according to the place in which it stands; and in like manner, a 2 is *two units*, or *two tens*, or *two hundreds*, &c. The same rule determines the value of each of the other figures.

In reading numbers, the units and tens are taken together. 1 ten and 1 unit are read *eleven;* 1 ten and 2 units, *twelve;* 1 ten and 3 units, *thirteen*, &c.: 2 tens and one unit are read *twenty-one;* 3 tens and 1 unit, *thirty-one*, &c. Thus the number expressed by the row of figures in table first is read—*one hundred and eleven millions, one hundred and eleven thousands, one hundred and eleven.* That expressed by the figures in table second is read—*two hundred and twenty-two millions, two hundred and twenty-two thousands, two hundred and twenty-two.*

The succeeding tables will further illustrate the subject.

TABLE THIRD.

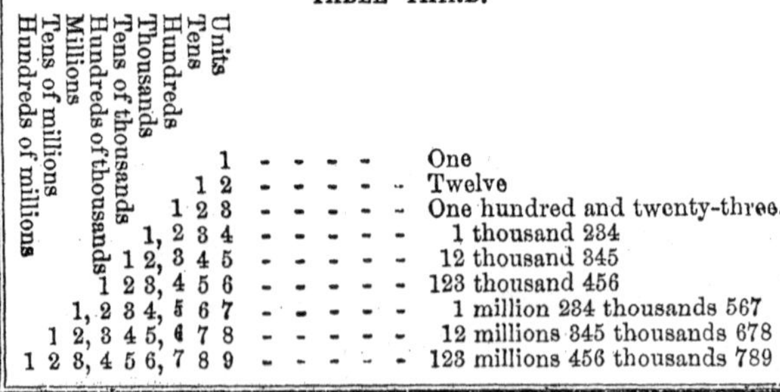

Hundreds of millions	Tens of millions	Millions	Hundreds of thousands	Tens of thousands	Thousands	Hundreds	Tens	Units		
								1	- - - -	One
							1	2	- - - - -	Twelve
						1	2	3	- - - - - -	One hundred and twenty-three.
					1,	2	3	4	- - - - - -	1 thousand 234
				1	2,	3	4	5	- - - - - -	12 thousand 345
			1	2	3,	4	5	6	- - - - - -	123 thousand 456
		1,	2	3	4,	5	6	7	- - - - - -	1 million 234 thousands 567
	1	2,	3	4	5,	6	7	8	- - - - - -	12 millions 345 thousands 678
1	2	3,	4	5	6,	7	8	9	- - - - - -	123 millions 456 thousands 789

In writing numbers which have no units, or no tens, or no hundreds, &c., the order observed in the foregoing tables must be maintained by filling the vacant places with a character called a nought or cypher, (0) which, of itself, represents no number. See

TABLE FOURTH.

Hundreds of millions	Tens of millions	Millions	Hundreds of thousands	Tens of thousands	Thousands	Hundreds	Tens	Units	
							1	0	- - Ten
						1	0	0	- - One hundred
					1,	0	0	0	- - 1 thousand
				1	0,	0	0	0	- - 10 thousand
			1	0	0,	0	0	0	- - 100 thousand
		1,	0	0	0,	0	0	0	- - 1 million
	1	0,	0	0	0,	0	0	0	- - 10 millions
1	0	0,	0	0	0,	0	0	0	- - 100 millions
2	0	0,	0	0	0,	0	0	2	- - 200 millions and 2
3	0	0,	0	0	3,	0	3	0	- - 300 millions 3 thou. and 30
4	0	4,	0	4	0,	4	0	0	- - 404 millions 40 thou. 4 hun.
5	5	0,	5	0	0,	0	0	0	- - 550 millions 500 thousand

EXAMPLES.

Read the following numbers, or write them in words.

Note.—Making a point or dot after every third figure, counting from the units place, greatly facilitates the reading of large numbers.

10, 11, 12, 13, 14, 15, 16, 17, 18, 19, 20, 21, 22, 30, 31, 32, 40, 43, 44, 50, 55, 56, 60, 67, 68, 70, 71, 79, 80, 82, 83, 90, 92, 100, 101, 111, 112, 113, 114, 120, 128, 130, 132, 200, 203, 210, 300, 320, 332, 400, 500, 600, 700, 800, 900, 1000, 2001, 3010, 4020, 5200, 10250, 23450, 356789, 6789402, 76450791, 20156789, 1304136784.

Write the following numbers in figures:

Ten. Twelve. Fifteen. Seventeen. Twenty-six. Thirty-nine. Fifty-two. Seventy-four. Eighty-one. Ninety-six. One hundred and fifteen. Two hundred. Three hundred and twenty. Nine hundred and nine. One thousand two hundred. Seven thousand seven hundred and thirty. One hundred and forty thousand. Seven hundred thousand five hundred and sixty-three. Seventeen millions. Eignty-four millions two thousand and forty-nine. Two hundred millions and fifteen.

SIMPLE ADDITION.

Addition teaches to collect several numbers into one.

The number formed by adding several numbers, is called the *amount* or *sum* of those numbers.

RULE.

Place the numbers one under another, with units under units, tens under tens, &c.; then, beginning with the units, add up all the columns successively, and under each column set down its amount. But if either of the amounts (except the last) be more than 9, set down its right hand figure only, and add the number expressed by its left hand figure or figures into the next column. The whole amount of the last column must be set down.

PROOF.

Perform the addition downwards.

EXAMPLES.

	4133	4832	5130
	4211	8523	4320
	3022	9743	406010
	8321	7244	207240
Amount	19687	30342	622700

1	2	12	24	41	80	123
3	3	13	36	60	90	322
2	4	20	41	70	70	231
1	5	30	90	50	60	202

964	804	670	701	20
375	670	950	300	37
412	942	100	204	431
566	820	200	702	560
719	170	320	500	290

1234	3220	4012	14004
3210	4500	5079	15604
1369	3721	9020	32009
4532	2904	2046	56005
5011	5800	3043	13208

7300	7300	16040
3211	24200	125100
25320	309220	676000
253221	1408000	2010000
131204	8060	21300000
105132	19000	10000000

Add the following numbers, viz: 14, 18, 99, 45, 28, 27, 19, 38, 16, 39, 48, 29, 260, 148.

Add, six hundred and forty, seventy-nine, eighty, one hundred, two hundred and ten, four hundred and fifty.

Add, nineteen thousands, fifty thousands, one million one hundred and one, one hundred and twenty-five.

APPLICATION.

1. If John give Charles twenty nuts, and James give him fifty-six, and Joseph give him ninety-five, how many will he have? Answer 171.

2. A person went to collect money, and received of one man ninety dollars; of another, one hundred and forty dollars; of another, one hundred and one dollars; and of another twenty-nine dollars. How much did he collect in all? Ans. 360 dollars.

3. Deposited in bank, fifty dollars in gold, three hundred dollars in silver, and five thousand dollars in notes. What is the whole amount deposited? Ans. 5350 dols.

4. The distance from Philadelphia to Bristol is 20 miles; from Bristol to Trenton, 10 miles; from Trenton to Princeton, 12 miles; from Princeton to Brunswick, 18 miles; from Brunswick to New York, 30 miles. How many miles from Philadelphia to New York? Ans. 90.

5. A merchant bought of one person 50 barrels of flour for 300 dollars; of another person, 75 barrels for 525 dollars; and of another person, 125 barrels for 1000

dollars. How many barrels did he buy, and how much did he pay for the whole?

Ans. 250 barrels, and paid 1825 dollars.

SIMPLE SUBTRACTION.

By Subtraction we ascertain how much greater one number is than another: or what remains when a less number is taken from a greater.

RULE.

Place the less number under the greater, with units under units, tens under tens, &c. Then, beginning at the units place, take each lower figure from the one above it, and set down what remains. But if either of the lower figures be greater than the upper one, conceive 10 to be added to the upper,* then take the lower from it, and set down the remainder. When 10 is thus added to the upper figure, there must be 1 added to the next lower figure.

PROOF.

Add the remainder to the less number, and their amount will be equal to the greater.

EXAMPLES.

From	2568	4421	541030076
Take	1326	3879	2000806
Remainder	1242	542	539029270

43	95	87	152	453	241
21	17	49	141	362	23

7642	2043	6504	1860	3206
6729	1703	304	950	107

32016	98700	500612	765040032
12045	25290	499521	7000302

* Some prefer taking the lower figure from 10, adding the remainder to the upper, and setting down their amount.

Take one hundred and fifty-six from three hundred and twenty-five.

Subtract fifteen thousands five hundred and nine from twenty thousands six hundred and fifty-four.

Subtract twenty-five from ten thousands.

APPLICATION.

1. Charles has thirty-two marbles, and John has twenty-five: how many has Charles more than John? Ans. 7.

2. William is seventeen years old, and James is nine: how much older is William than James? Ans. 8 years.

3. Charles had twenty-five apples, but gave his brother twelve of them: how many had he left? Ans. 13.

4. A person had in bank 9000 pounds, but drew out 1112 pounds; how much money had he remaining in bank? Ans. 7888 pounds.

5. My friend owed me one hundred and fifty dollars, but has paid me ninety dollars: how much does he still owe me? Ans. 60 dollars.

ADDITION AND SUBTRACTION.

1. If I add 500, 627, and 1000, and subtract from their amount 900, what number will remain? Ans. 1227.

2. A person borrowed of me, at one time, 62 dollars; at another time, 150 dollars; and at another time, 200 dollars. He has now paid me 300 dollars. How much does he still owe me? Ans. 112 dollars.

3. Subtract 267 from 345, and add 150 to the remainder. Facit 228.

4. A person had in his desk 1000 dollars. He took out 120 dollars to pay a debt. He afterwards put in 75 dollars. How much was there then in the desk? Ans. 955 dollars.

SIMPLE MULTIPLICATION.

Multiplication teaches to find what a number amounts to when repeated a given number of times.

The number to be multiplied is called the *multiplicand.*

The number to multiply by is called the *multiplier.*

The number produced by multiplying is called the *product.*

The multiplier and multiplicand are also called *factors.*

☞ The scholar should commit the following Table to memory before he proceeds further.

MULTIPLICATION TABLE.

Twice		3 times		4 times		5 times		6 times		7 times	
1 make	2	1 make	3	1 make	4	1 make	5	1 make	6	1 make	7
2	4	2	6	2	8	2	10	2	12	2	14
3	6	3	9	3	12	3	15	3	18	3	21
4	8	4	12	4	16	4	20	4	24	4	28
5	10	5	15	5	20	5	25	5	30	5	35
6	12	6	18	6	24	6	30	6	36	6	42
7	14	7	21	7	28	7	35	7	42	7	49
8	16	8	24	8	32	8	40	8	48	8	56
9	18	9	27	9	36	9	45	9	54	9	63
10	20	10	30	10	40	10	50	10	60	10	70
11	22	11	33	11	44	11	55	11	66	11	77
12	24	12	36	12	48	12	60	12	72	12	84

8 times		9 times		10 times		11 times		12 times	
1 make	8	1 make	9	1 make	10	1 make	11	1 make	12
2	16	2	18	2	20	2	22	2	24
3	24	3	27	3	30	3	33	3	36
4	32	4	36	4	40	4	44	4	48
5	40	5	45	5	50	5	55	5	60
6	48	6	54	6	60	6	66	6	72
7	56	7	63	7	70	7	77	7	84
8	64	8	72	8	80	8	88	8	96
9	72	9	81	9	90	9	99	9	108
10	80	10	90	10	100	10	110	10	120
11	88	11	99	11	110	11	121	11	132
12	96	12	108	12	120	12	132	12	144

When the multiplier does not exceed 12, work by

RULE I.

Set the multiplier under the right hand figure or figures of the multiplicand. Then, beginning with the units, multiply all the figures of the multiplicand, in succession, and set down the several products. But if either of the products (except the last) be more than 9, set down its right hand figure only, and add its left hand figure or figures to the next product.—The whole of the last product must be set down.

PROOF.

Multiply by double the multiplier, and the product will be double the former product.

EXAMPLES.

Multiplicand	243	274	20052	40092
Multiplier	2	3	4	12
Product	486	822	80208	481104

12	38	60	112	245	209
2	3	4	3	6	2

2110	6690	9008	1992	1301
7	8	9	10	6

48732	97990	84605	340099
3	12	10	12

6707053	46214409	560420009
2	11	9

When the multiplier exceeds 12, work by

RULE II.

Multiply by each figure of the multiplier separately, first by the one at the right hand then by the next, and so on, placing their respective products one under another, with the right hand figure of each product directly under that figure of the multiplier by which it is produced. Add these products together; and their amount will be the product required.

Note.—When cyphers occur at the right hand of either or both of the factors, omit them in the operation, and annex them to the product.

EXAMPLES.

Multiplicand	26043	20432 | 0
Multiplier	432	5072 | 00
	52086	40864
	78129	143024
	104172	102160
Product	11250576	103631104 | 000

3. Multiply	25	by	13	Facit	325
4. —	125	by	36	—	4500
5. —	5231	by	145	—	758495
6. —	129186	by	98	—	12660228
7. —	23430	by	230	—	5388900
8. —	756	by	2000	—	1512000
9. —	5400420	by	23000	—	124209660000
10. —	674200	by	2104	—	1418516800
11. —	5401	by	300400	—	1622460400

Note.—When the multiplier is the exact product of any two factors in the multiplication table, the operation may be performed thus: multiply by one of the factors, and then multiply the number produced by the other factor.

EXAMPLES.

Muitiply 3412 by 21

	3412	3412
	3	7
	10236	23884
	7	3
Product	71652	Product 71652

3. Multiply	43102	by	66	Facit	2844732
4. —	12071	by	99	—	1195029
5. —	871075	by	42	—	36585150
6. —	526473	by	144	—	75812112

APPLICATION.

1. Richard has 125 nuts, and George has 6 times that number. How many has George? Ans. 750.

2. There are 20 boxes of raisins with 14 pounds in

each box. How many pounds are there in all? Ans. 280.

3. The price of one orange is 9 cents; how many cents will 5 oranges come to, at the same price? Ans. 45.

4. There are 12 pence in one shilling. How many pence are there in 40 shillings? Ans. 480.

ADDITION AND MULTIPLICATION.

1. Multiply 25 by 10, and 36 by 14, and 124 by 45. Add the several products, and tell their amount. Ans. 6334.

2. There are ten bags of coffee weighing each 120 pounds; and 12 bags weighing each 135 pounds. What is the weight of the whole? Ans. 2820 pounds.

3. A merchant bought five pieces of linen containing 25 yards each, and 2 pieces containing 24 yards each, and 1 piece containing 26 yards. How many yards were there in the whole? Ans. 199.

SUBTRACTION AND MULTIPLICATION.

1. Multiply 342 by 22, and from the product subtract 400. Facit 7124.

2. There are 15 bags of coffee, each of which weighs 112 pounds. The bags which contain the coffee weigh 22 pounds. How much would the coffee weigh without the bags? Ans. 1658 pounds.

3. There are 12 chests of tea, each of which weighs 96 pounds. The chests which contain the tea weigh each 20 pounds. What would the tea weigh without the chests? Ans. 912 pounds.

DIVISION.

By division we ascertain how often one number is contained in another.

The number to be divided is called the *dividend.*

The number to divide by is called the *divisor.*

The number of times the dividend contains the divisor is called the *quotient.*

If, on dividing a number, there be any overplus, it is called the *remainder.*

The *dividual* is a partial dividend, or so many of the dividend figures as are taken to be divided at one time, and which produce one quotient figure.

When the divisor does not exceed 12, work by

RULE I.

See how often the divisor is contained in the first left hand figure or figures of the dividend.* If it be contained an exact number of times, set down that number; and then see how often it is contained in the next figure. But if it be contained any number of times with a remainder, set down the number of times, and conceive the remainder to be prefixed to the next figure; then see how often the divisor is contained in these, and proceed as before till the whole is divided

PROOF.

Multiply the quotient by the divisor, and to their product add the remainder, (if any,) and the result will be equal to the dividend.

EXAMPLES.

	Dividend			
Divisor	3)963	5)2960	12)112813	12)970811280
Quotient	321	592	9401+1	80900940

2)864   4)1416   5)56160   6)12180

12)115218   8)7284016   3)9635410

12)850811550   9)24600134   11)405320004

11. Divide 46323 by 9 Facit 5147
12. ——— 1430400 by 7 —— 204342 Rem. 6.
13. ——— 6730214 by 10 —— 673021 —— 4.

* The multiplication table shows how often any number, not exceeding 12, is contained in any other number not exceeding 144; as that 4 is contained in 12 *three* times, because 3 times 4 are 12; 10 is contained in 115 *eleven* times with 5 over; because 11 times 10 are 110, which, with 5, make 115.

When the divisor exceeds 12, work by

RULE II. OF

LONG DIVISION.

Take for the first dividual as few of the left hand figures of the dividend as will contain the divisor, try how often they will contain it, and set the number of times on the right of the dividend—multiply the divisor by this number—subtract its product from the dividual, and to the remainder affix the next figure of the dividend, to form a second dividual: or if this be not sufficient, set a cypher on the right of the dividend, and affix the next figure, and so on, till a sufficient number of figures are affixed—try how often the divisor is contained in this second dividual, and proceed as before. Continue this process till all the dividend figures are employed as above directed; or till the number they form, when affixed to a remainder, is not large enough to contain the divisor.

When the work is done, the figures on the right of the dividend form the quotient.

PROOF.—As under Rule I.

EXAMPLES.

```
                         Divisor  Dividend     Quotient
42)9870(235                  320)12864016081(40200050
   84                            1280
   ---                           ----
   147                             640
   126                             640
   ---                             ----
    210                             1608
    210                             1600
    ---                             ----
                             Remainder 81
```

1.	Divide	4633	by	41	Facit	113		
2.	—	2303	by	49	—	47		
3.	—	465	by	27	—	17	Rem.	6
4.	—	40231	by	75	—	536	—	31
5.	—	253622	by	422	—	601		
6.	—	13699840	by	342	—	40058	—	4
7.	—	4586841	by	3467	—	1323		
8.	—	46447786	by	1234	—	37640	—	26

Note 1.—Cyphers on the right of the divisor may be omitted in the operation, observing to separate as many figures from the right of the dividend, which annex to the remainder.

EXAMPLES.

1. Divide 146340 by 5400. Facit 27, remainder 540.

```
54|00)1463|40(27
      108
      ---
       383
       378
       ---
        540
        ---
```

2. Divide	76173	by	320	Facit	238	Rem.	13
3. —	867894	by	300	—	2892	—	294
4. —	15463420	by	1600	—	9664	—	1020
5. —	99607765	by	27000	—	3689	—	4765
6. —	1345680000	by	120000	—	11214		

Note 2.—When the divisor is the exact product of any two factors in the multiplication table, the division may be performed thus:—Divide first by one of the factors agreeably to Rule I.; then divide the quotient by the other factor in the same manner.

When a remainder occurs in the first operation and none in the last, it is the true one: but a remainder in the last operation must be multiplied by the first divisor, and its product added to the first remainder (if any) for the true remainder.

EXAMPLES.

1. Divide 46508974 by 96. Facit 484468. Rem. 46.

```
 8)46508974
   --------
12)5813621—6 first remainder.
   --------
    484468—5 last remainder.
           8
           —
          40
           6
           —
          46 true remainder.
```

2. Divide	34320	by 99	Facit	346	Rem.	66
3. —	20208	by 48	—	421		
4. —	5704392	by 108	—	52818	—	48

APPLICATION.

1. As division is a short method of discovering how often one number is contained in another, how often is 3 contained in 3699? Ans. 1233 times.

2. How many times is 25 contained in 132? Ans. 5 times with 7 over.

3. There are 12 pence in one shilling. How many shillings are there in 480 pence? Ans. 40.

4. The price of a pair of shoes is 2 dollars. How many pair may be had for 56 dollars? Ans. 28.

5. Fifty-four apples are to be divided equally between 2 boys. How many must each boy have? Ans. 27.

6. Suppose a man travel 40 miles a day: how many days will he be in travelling 240 miles? Ans. 6.

ADDITION AND DIVISION.

1. If I add 167, 394, and 447; and divide their amount by 12: what number will result? Ans. 84.

2. A person has in money 5000 dollars; in bank-stock, 3500 dollars; and in merchandize 12500 dollars. He intends to divide this property equally among his 3 sons. What will be the share of each son? Ans. 7000 dollars.

3. Suppose a farmer, who has a plantation of 520 acres, buys an adjoining one of 375 acres, and divides the whole into five equal portions: how many acres will there be in each portion? Ans. 179.

SUBTRACTION AND DIVISION.

1. Subtract 2468 from 5796, and divide the remainder by 26. Result 128.

2. William bought 12 pears: he kept 6 of them, and divided the rest between his two sisters. How many did each sister receive? Ans. 3.

3. A man, at his decease, left property amounting to 12426 pounds. He directed in his will that 1000 pounds should be given to his niece; and that the

remainder of the property should be divided equally between his two nephews. What is the share of each nephew? Ans. 5713 pounds.

MULTIPLICATION AND DIVISION.

1. Multiply 145 by 12, and divide the product by 6. Result 290.

2. To find how many dollars are contained in any number of pounds, we multiply the pounds by 8, and divide their product by 3. How many dollars are there in 456 pounds? Ans. 1216.

3. To find how many pounds are contained in any number of dollars, we multiply the dollars by 3, and divide their product by 8. How many pounds are there in 8576 dollars? Ans. 3216.

FEDERAL MONEY,

OR MONEY OF THE UNITED STATES.

The denominations of Federal Money are; Eagle, Dollar, Dime, Cent, and Mill.

10 mills (*m.*) make 1 cent, *cts.*
10 cents — 1 dime.
10 dimes (or 100 *cts.* 1 dollar, *D.* or $.
10 dollars — 1 eagle.

These denominations have precisely the same relative values as those of unit, ten, hundred, &c., and are also similarly ranged in Numeration. Federal money is therefore added, subtracted, multiplied, and divided by the same rules that are given for Simple Addition, Subtraction, Multiplication, and Division.

It must be remarked, however, that in writing sums of Federal Money, parts of a cent are generally used instead of mills; and that, in reading those sums, neither the eagles nor dimes are mentioned: the former being considered as tens of dollars; and the latter as tens of cents.

The parts or fractions of a cent, used instead of mills, are expressed by two numbers, placed one above the other, with a line drawn between them. The under number denotes the part; and the upper one informs how many of that part are designed to be expressed: as,

$\frac{1}{4}$ one fourth; $\frac{3}{4}$ three fourths; $\frac{1}{3}$ one third; $\frac{2}{3}$ two thirds; $\frac{1}{2}$ a half.

NUMERATION OF FEDERAL MONEY.

In writing sums of Federal Money, the cents are placed on the right of the dollars, and are separated from them by a point. If there are not more than nine cents in the sum, a cypher is put in the tens' place; and if there are no cents, two cyphers are used.

If the point which separates the dollars from the cents be removed or supposed to be removed, the sum may be considered as cents only: and when the sum is cents only, if two figures be separated from the right, all on the left of these will be dollars. See the following

TABLE.

Thousands of dollars	Hundreds of dollars	Eagles or tens of dollars	Dollars		Dimes or tens of cents	Cents	
			1	,	3	4	. . 1 dol. 34 cents, or 134 cents
		1	2	,	1	0	. 12 dols. 10 cents, or 1210 cents
		2	3	,	2	0	. 23 dols. 20 cents, or 2320 cents
	5	6	0	,	0	7	. 560 dols. 7 cents, or 56007 cents
	6	4	2	,	0	6$\frac{1}{4}$	. 642 dols. 6 cts. and $\frac{1}{4}$, or 64206$\frac{1}{4}$ c.
6	0	0	4	,	1	2$\frac{1}{2}$	6004 dols. 12 cts. and $\frac{1}{2}$, or 600412$\frac{1}{2}$ c.
9	1	2	6	,	1	8$\frac{3}{4}$	9126 dols. 18 cts. and $\frac{3}{4}$, or 912618$\frac{3}{4}$ c.

EXAMPLES.

To be read by the learner as dollars and cents, and also as cents only.

1.49 3.26 4.75 9.18 17.90 21.09 14.02
125.00 426.00 900.00 340.06$\frac{1}{4}$ 3911.10$\frac{1}{4}$ 4006.18$\frac{3}{4}$
76420.01 19560.00 11904.10$\frac{1}{3}$ 4896.73$\frac{2}{3}$ 400.00$\frac{1}{4}$
4500.06$\frac{1}{4}$.

The following to be written in figures:

Seventeen dollars and fifty-two cents. Forty-nine dollars and seventeen cents. Eighty-four dollars and ten cents. Sixty dollars and twelve and a half cents. Two hundred and fourteen dollars and six cents and a half. Three hundred dollars. One thousand dollars. Seven thousand dollars and four cents.

ADDITION OF FEDERAL MONEY.

RULE.

Place the sums one under another, with dollars under dollars and cents under cents; then, if there are no fractions, proceed in the same manner as in Simple Addition, observing to separate the cents of the amount from the dollars thereof, by placing a point between them. When fractions occur, find their amount in fourths;* consider how many cents these fourths will make; add them with the cents in the right hand column, and proceed as before directed.

Proof; as in Simple Addition.

Note.—To find how many cents there are in any number of fourths of a cent, divide them by 4, and the quotient will be cents.

EXAMPLES.

D.	*cts.*	*m.*		*D.*	*cts.*		*D.*	*cts.*
40	15	5		42	06			$18\frac{3}{4}$
21	10	0		156	20		4	$12\frac{1}{2}$
46	12	8		340	59		89	$06\frac{1}{4}$
20	09	4		250	25		2140	00
50	17	2		200	00		4000	50
$ 177	64	9		989	10		6233	$87\frac{1}{2}$

---

* In Addition, Subtraction, and Division of Federal Money, all fractions less than a fourth are omitted, and every fraction greater than a fourth is reckoned a half, three fourths, or a whole cent, according to its value: so that in these three operations, no fractions are used excepting fourths—a half being counted two fourths. But in Multiplication it is often material that no fraction be omitted, and that all fractions should be estimated at their real value.

D	cts.	m.	D.	cts.	D.	cts.	D.	cts.
5	40	2	21	14	140	06¼	1	18¾
4	10	0	56	10	350	19	12	56¼
3	12	5	95	75	200	00	45	12½
5	04	2	56	15	350	08	145	12½
2	95	1	88	15	520	12½	3500	18¾
$								

8 Add the following sums; viz., 45 dollars; 156 dollars: 1000 dollars, and 750 dollars.

9 Add 48 dollars 20 cents; 14 dollars 58 cents; 100 dollars, and 500 dollars.

10. Add 4 cents; 10 cents; 55 cents; 15 cents, and 11 cents.

11. Add 12½ cents; 18¾ cents; 56¼ cents; 20 cents; 95 cents, and 42 cents.

APPLICATION.

1. Bought a hat for 4 dollars; a pair of shoes for 2 dollars 25 cents; a pair of stockings for 1 dollar 50 cents; and a pair of gloves for 75 cents. What is the cost of the whole? Ans. 8 dollars 50 cents.

2. Bought a Bible for 1 dollar; an English Reader for 75 cents; an Introduction for 50 cents; a slate for 31¼ cents; a slate pencil for 1 cent; and a copy book for 12½ cents. How much do they all amount to? Ans. 2 dollars 69¾ cents.

3. Suppose I buy a barrel of sugar for 30 dollars 87½ cents; a bag of coffee for 22 dollars 18¾ cents; and a bushel of salt for 1 dollar 12½ cents: what sum must I pay for the whole? Ans. 54 dollars 18¾ cents.

SUBTRACTION OF FEDERAL MONEY.

RULE.

Place the less sum under the greater, with dollars under dollars, cents under cents, &c.: then if there are no fractions, proceed as in Simple Subtraction; observing to separate the dollars from the cents, in the remainder. If there is a fraction in the upper sum, and none in the lower, set it down as part of the remainder, and proceed as before directed. If there is a fraction in each of the sums, and the lower less than the upper, subtract the lower from the upper, and set down the difference. If there is a fraction in the lower sum, and none in the upper, subtract it from 4, and set down the difference: in this case there must be 1 added to the right hand figure of the cents, in the lower sum, before it is subtracted from the one above it. If there is a fraction in each of the sums, and the lower greater than the upper, subtract the lower from 4, add the difference to the upper, and set down the amount. In this case, as in the last, there must be 1 added to the right hand figure of the lower cents.

Proof; as in Simple Subtraction.

EXAMPLES.

	D. cts. m.	*D. cts.*	*D. cts.*	*D. cts.*
	54 , 67 , 5	56 , 75	35 , 18$\frac{3}{4}$	25 , 18$\frac{3}{4}$
	40 , 01 , 2	41 , 25	21 , 10	14 , 22$\frac{1}{2}$
$	14 , 66 , 3	15 , 50	14 , 08$\frac{3}{4}$	10 , 96$\frac{1}{4}$

	D. cts.	*D. cts.*	*D. cts. m.*	*D. cts.*
	65 , 49	520 , 31$\frac{1}{4}$	14 , 07 , 6	35 , 20
	55 , 14$\frac{1}{4}$	210 , 12$\frac{1}{2}$	9 , 10 , 8	14 , 12
$	10 , 34$\frac{3}{4}$	310 , 18$\frac{3}{4}$		

	D. cts.	*D. cts.*	*D. cts.*	*D. cts.*
	35 , 12$\frac{1}{2}$	49 , 18$\frac{3}{4}$	50 , 00	456 , 45$\frac{1}{2}$
	22 , 00	20 , 06$\frac{1}{4}$	20 , 12$\frac{1}{2}$	451 , 20$\frac{3}{4}$
$				

13. Subtract 456 dollars from 1000 dollars.
14. Subtract 45 cents from 64 cents.
15. Subtract 375 dollars 18 cents from 400 dollars.

APPLICATION.

1. Bought goods to the amount of 545 dollars 95 cents, and paid at the time of purchase, 350 dollars. How much remains to be paid? Ans. 195 dols. 95 cts.

2. A merchant bought a quantity of coffee, for which he paid 560 dollars. He afterwards sold it for 610 dol-

lars $87\frac{1}{2}$ cents. How much did he gain by the transaction? Ans. 50 dollars $87\frac{1}{2}$ cents.

3. If a storekeeper seells goods for 102 dollars, which cost 125 dollars 75 cents: how much will he lose by the sale? Ans. 23 dollars 75 cents.

MULTIPLICATION OF FEDERAL MONEY.

RULE.

Set the multiplier under the sum to be multiplied: then, if there is no fraction, proceed as in Simple Multiplication: observing to separate the cents from the dollars in the product. If there is a fraction in the sum, multiply it, and find how many cents are contained in its product: then multiply the cents of the sum, and add to their product the cents contained in the product of the fraction, and proceed as before directed. Or, if the multiplier exceed 12, multiply the sum, omitting the fraction: then multiply the fraction, and add the number of cents contained in its product to the product of the rest of the sum.

Proof: as in Simple Multiplication.

Note.—To multiply a fraction of a cent, and find how many cents are contained in its product—multiply the upper number of the fraction, and divide its product by the under one, and the result will be the number of cents.

EXAMPLES.

D. *cts.*	*D.* *cts.*	*D.* *cts.*	*D.* *cts.*
12 , 50	10 , $56\frac{1}{4}$	140 , $18\frac{2}{3}$	10 , $87\frac{1}{2}$
4	2	10	125
50 , 00	21 , $12\frac{1}{2}$	1401 , $86\frac{2}{3}$	5435
			2174
			1087
			$62\frac{1}{2}$
			1359,$37\frac{1}{2}$

D. *cts.* *m.*	*D.* *cts.*	*D.* *cts.*
9 , 10 , 3	12 , 75	145 , $18\frac{3}{4}$
2	4	7

					D. cts.
8.	Multiply	$500	by 4	Product	2000,00
9.	———	$42 56¼ cts.	by 3	———	127,68¾
10.	———	25 cts.	by 3	———	75
11.	———	37½ cts.	by 5	———	1,87½
12.	———	$4 18¾ cts.	by 12	———	50,25
13.	———	$10 33⅓ cts.	by 10	———	103,33⅓
14.	———	$5 66⅔ cts.	by 20	———	113,33⅓
15.	———	$29 38 cts.	by 96	———	2820,48
16.	———	$102 19 cts.	by 120	———	12262,80
17.	———	$31 17½ cts.	by 208	———	6484,40
18.	———	$25 18¾ cts.	by 25	———	629,68¾

APPLICATION.

1. How much will 11 oranges come to, at 12½ cents each? Ans. 1 dol. 37½ cts.

2. What will 10 loaves of bread come to, at 6¼ cents a loaf? Ans. 62½ cts.

3. What will 8 cords of wood amount to, at 4 dollars 50 cents a cord? Ans. 36 dollars.

4. Sold 213 barrels of flour, for 6 dollars 25 cents per barrel. What is the amount? Ans. 1331 dols. 25 cts.

5. Bought 308 pounds of coffee at 21 cents a pound. What is the amount? Ans. 64 dols. 68 cts.

6. How much will 132 pieces of linen come to, at 17 dollars 37½ cents each? Ans. 2293 dols. 50 cts.

DIVISION OF FEDERAL MONEY.

RULE.

Divide as in Simple Division. When a remainder occurs, multiply it by 4, and add the number of fourths that are in the fraction of the sum (if any) to its product: divide this product by the divisor, and its quotient will be fourths; which annex to the quotient of the sum.

Proof: as in Simple division.

EXAMPLES.

```
  D.  cts       D.  cts.          D.     cts. D.    cts.
2)45 , 22     3)63 , 18¾      25)629 , 68¾(25  18¾
                                 50
  22 , 61       21 , 06¼        ---
                                 129
                                 125
  D.  cts.      D.    cts.  m.   ---
8)85 , 00    12)740 , 41 , 2      46
                                  25
  10 , 62½      61 , 70 , 1      ---
                                  218
                                  200
  D.  cts.      D.   cts.  m.     ---
4)25 , 24    11)56 , 50 , 7        18
                                    4
                                   --
                                 25)75(3 fourths.
                                    75
```

					D. cts.
8. Divide	56 dols. 15 cts.	by	10	Quotient	5,61½
9. ——	96 dols.	by	5	——	19,20
10. ——	156 dols.	by	4	——	39,00
11. ——	346 dols.	by	8	——	43,25
12. ——	1465 dols. 92½ cts.	by	2	——	732,96¼
13. ——	500 dols. 73¾ cts.	by	9	——	55,63¾
14. ——	58 dols. 14 cts.	by	38	——	1,53
15. ——	417 dols. 96 cts.	by	129	——	3,24
16. ——	7550 dols.	by	125	——	60,40
17. ——	4640 dols. 18¾ cts.	by	15	——	309,34½
18. ——	28 dols. 80 cts.	by	360	——	8

APPLICATION.

1. To divide 52 dollars 68 cents, equally, among 6 persons, what sum must be given to each ? Ans. 8 dols. 78 cents.

2. If 8 pounds of coffee cost 2 dollars 4 cents, what is the price of 1 pound ? Ans. 25½ cts.

3. Bought 29 yards of fine linen for 65 dollars 25 cts. What was the price per yard ? Ans. 2 dols. 25 cts.

4. Paid 58 dollars 75 cents for 235 yards of muslin. What was it per yard ? Ans. 25 cts.

5. If 103 bushels of wheat cost 225 dollars 57 cents; how much is it a bushel? Ans. 2 dols. 19 cts.

6. Sold 144 yards of fine linen for 90 dollars. How much is that per yard? Ans. 62½ cts.

PROMISCUOUS EXAMPLES.

1. If I add the following sums, viz. 556 dollars 18¾ cents; 825 dollars 12½ cents; and 1000 dollars; and subtract from their amount 125 dollars: what sum will result? Ans. 2256 dols. 31¼ cts.

2. If I subtract 125 dollars 18¾ cents from 456 dollars 75 cents, and multiply the remainder by 4, what sum will result? Ans. 1326 dols. 25 cts.

3. A person has 200 dollars. He owes his tailor 65 dollars 87½ cents; his shoemaker, 25 dollars 75 cents; and his hatter, 18 dollars. What sum will he have remaining, after paying these debts? Ans. 90 dols. 37½ cts.

4. Purchased 10 bushels of potatoes at 56¼ cents per bushel; 2 bushels of corn at 87½ cents per bushel; and 2 barrels of flour at 8 dollars per barrel. What is the amount of the whole? Ans. 23 dols. 37½ cts.

5. Calculate the amount of articles in the following bill:

J. Jones, Bought of S. Smith,

		D.	*cts.*	
19 yards of lace, -	at	2 ,	37½	per yard
14 yards of ribbon,	at		18¾	———
24 ditto ditto	at		25	———
8 pair of gloves,	at		27	per pair
13 fans, - - - - -	at		13½	each
2 pair of knots, -	at		25	per pair

Amount $ 58 , 16½ cts.

SIMPLE REDUCTION.

Reduction is the changing of a sum or quantity, from one denomination to another, without increasing or lessening its value.

Simple reduction is the reducing of sums or quantities which have but a single denomination.

When a sum or quantity is to be changed to a lower denomination than its own, work by

RULE: *

Multiply the sum or quantity by that number of the lower denomination which makes one of its own.† (See notes 1, 2, and 3.)

If there are one or more denominations between the denomination of the given sum or quantity, and that to which it is to be changed: first change it to the next lower than its own, and then to the next lower, and so on. See notes 4 and 5.

ENGLISH MONEY.

The denominations of English Money are pound, shilling, penny, and farthing.

4 farthings (*qr.*)	make	1 penny	*d.*
12 pence	- - - -	1 shilling	*s.*
20 shillings	- - - -	1 pound	£.

☞ Farthings are written as fractions, thus:

$\frac{1}{4}$ one farthing.
$\frac{1}{2}$ two farthings, or a halfpenny.
$\frac{3}{4}$ three farthings.

EXAMPLES.

Note 1.—*To reduce pounds to shillings, multiply them by* 20, *because every pound makes* 20 *shillings.*

Reduce 15 pounds to shillings. Facit 300 shillings.

```
 15
 20
---
300 shillings.
```

2. Reduce 256 pounds to shillings. Facit 5120 s.

---

* The reason of this rule is plain: for if it take twenty shillings to make one pound, it must take 5 times 20 shillings to make 5 pounds; and to find how many 5 times twenty are, we may either multiply 20 by 5, or 5 by twenty. Likewise, if it take 4 pecks to make one bushel, it must take 6 times 4 pecks to make 6 bushels, &c.

† One denomination is said to be *lower* than another, when it is of less value; and *higher*, when it is of greater value: thus a shilling is a lower denomination than a pound; and a higher denomination than a penny.

Note 2.—*To reduce shillings to pence, multiply them by* 12, *because every shilling makes* 12 *pence.*

3. Reduce 60 shillings to pence. Facit 720 d.
4. Bring 120 shillings to pence. Facit 1440 d

Note 3.—*To reduce pence to farthings, multiply them by* 4, *because every penny makes* 4 *farthings.*

5. Reduce 350 pence to farthings. Facit 1400 qrs.
6. Change 4560 pence to farthings. Facit 18240 qrs.

Note 4.—*To reduce shillings to farthings, change them first to pence, and then change those pence to farthings.*

7. Reduce 10 shillings to farthings. Facit 480 qrs.
8. Bring 115 shillings to farthings. Facit 5520 qrs.

Note 5.—*To reduce pounds to farthings, reduce them first to shillings; then change those shillings to pence; and then change those pence to farthings.*

9. Reduce 5 pounds to farthings. Facit 4800 qrs.
10. Bring 76 pounds to farthings. Facit 72960 qrs.

FEDERAL MONEY.

☞ The denominations of Federal Money have already been given.

EXAMPLES.

Note 1.—*To reduce dollars to cents, multiply them by* 100; *or, which is the same thing, annex two cyphers to their number.*

1. Reduce fifty dollars to cents. Facit 5000 cts.
2. Reduce 125 dollars to cents. Facit 12500 cts.
3. Bring 5560 dollars to cents. Facit 556000 cts.

Note 2.—*To reduce cents to fourths or quarters of a cent, multiply them by* 4;—*to halves, multiply them by* 2;—*to thirds, multiply them by* 3, *&c.*

4. Reduce 25 cents to fourths or quarters of a cent. Facit 100 fourths.
5. Reduce 256 cents to fourths of a cent. Facit 1024 fourths.
6. Reduce 45 cents to half cents. Facit 90 halves.
7. Bring 145 cents to thirds of a cent. Facit 435 thirds.

Note 3.—*To reduce dollars to fourths, halves, or thirds of a cent, &c.—first bring them to cents; and then bring those cents to fourths, or halves, &c.*

8. Reduce 12 dollars to fourths of a cent.
Facit 4800 fourths.

9. Bring 122 dollars to halves of a cent.
Facit 24400 halves.

10. Bring 54 dollars to thirds of a cent.
Facit 16200 thirds.

Note 4.—*To reduce dollars to mills, multiply them by* 1000; *or, which is the same thing, annex three cyphers to their number.*

11. Reduce 26 dollars to mills. Facit 26000 *m.*

12. Bring 150 dollars to mills. Facit 150000 *m.*

AVOIRDUPOIS WEIGHT.

By this weight are weighed things of a coarse, drossy nature, that are bought and sold by weight, and all metals but silver and gold.

The denominations of Avoirdupois Weight are ton, hundred weight, quarter, pound, ounce, and dram.

16 drams (*dr.*) make	1 ounce - -	*oz.*
16 ounces - - -	1 pound - -	*lb.*
28 pounds - -	1 quarter of a cwt.	*qr.*
4 quarters, or 112 lb.	1 hundred weight	*C.wt.*
20 hundred weight	1 ton - - - -	*T.*

EXAMPLES.

1. Reduce 27 tons to a hundred weights. Facit 540 *C.wt.*
2. Bring 45 hundred weight to quarters. Facit 180 *qr.*
3. Bring 250 quarters to pounds. Facit 7000 *lb.*
4. Reduce 76 pounds to ounces. Facit 1216 *oz.*
5. Bring 40 ounces to drams. Facit 640 drams.
6. Reduce 8 tons to pounds. Facit 17920 *lb.*
7. Bring 2 tons to drams. Facit 1146880 *dr.*

TROY WEIGHT.

By this weight jewels, gold, silver, and liquors are weighed.

The denominations of Troy Weight are pound, ounce, pennyweight, and grain.

24 grains (*gr.*) make	1 pennyweight	*dwt.*
20 pennyweights -	1 ounce	*oz.*
12 ounces -	1 pound	*lb.*

EXAMPLES.

1. Reduce 576 pounds to ounces. Facit 6912 *oz.*

2. Change 1740 ounces to pennyweights. Facit 34800 *dwts.*
3. Bring 145 pennyweights to grains. Facit 3480 *gr.*
4. Reduce 15 pounds to pennyweights. Facit 3600 *dwts.*
5. Bring 75 pounds to grains. Facit 432000 *gr.*

APOTHECARIES' WEIGHT.

By this weight apothecaries mix their medicines, but buy and sell by avoirdupois weight.

The denominations of Apothecaries' Weight are pound, ounce, dram, scruple, and grain.

20 grains (*gr.*)	make	1	scruple	℈
3 scruples	- -	1	dram	ʒ
8 drams	- -	1	ounce	℥
12 ounces	- -	1	pound	℔

EXAMPLES.

1. Reduce 56 pounds to ounces. Facit 672 ℥
2. Reduce 142 ounces to drams. Facit 1136 ʒ
3. Bring 84 drams to scruples. Facit 252 ℈
4. Bring 16 scruples to grains. Facit 320 *gr.*
5. Reduce 8 ounces to scruples. Facit 192 ℈
6. Bring 14 pounds to grains. Facit 80640 *gr.*

LONG MEASURE.

Long Measure is used for lengths and distances.

The denominations of Long Measure are degree, league, mile, furlong, pole, yard, foot, and inch.

12 inches (*in.*) make	-	1	foot - - -	*ft.*
3 feet - - -	-	1	yard - -	*yd.*
5½ yards - -	-	1	rod, pole, or perch	*P.*
40 poles (or 220 yds.)	-	1	furlong -	*fur.*
8 furlongs (or 1760 yds.)		1	mile - - -	*M.*
3 miles - -	-	1	league - - -	*L.*
60 geographic, or 69½ statute } miles		1	degree - -	*deg.*

Note.—A hand is a measure of 4 inches, and used in measuring the height of horses.

A fathom is 6 feet, and used chiefly in measuring the depth of water.

EXAMPLES.

1. Reduce 20 leagues to miles. Facit 60 *m.*

2. Reduce 75 miles to furlongs. Facit 600 *fur.*
3. Bring 42 furlongs to poles. Facit 1680 *P.*
4. Bring 50 poles to yards. Facit 275 *yd.*
5. Bring 16 yards to feet. Facit 48 *ft.*
6. Bring 49 feet to inches. Facit 588 *in.*
7. Bring 10 yards to inches. Facit 360 *in.*
8. Reduce 3 leagues to poles. Facit 2880 *P.*

CLOTH MEASURE.

By this measure cloth, tapes, &c., are measured.

The denominations of Cloth Measure are English ell, Flemish ell, yard, quarter of a yard, and nail.

4 nails (*na.*)	make	1	quarter of a yard	*qr.*
4 quarters	- -	1	yard - -	*yd.*
3 quarters	- -	1	ell Flemish -	*E. Fl.*
5 quarters	- -	1	ell English -	*E. E.*

EXAMPLES.

1. Reduce 46 English ells to quarters. Facit 230 *qr.*
2. Bring 5 Flemish ells to quarters. Facit 15 *qr.*
3. Bring 22 yards to quarters. Facit 88 *qr.*
4. Bring 40 quarters to nails. Facit 160 *na.*
5. Bring 51 English ells to nails. Facit 1020 *na.*

LAND MEASURE, OR SQUARE MEASURE.

This measure shows the quantity of lands.

The denominations of Land Measure are acre, rood square perch, square yard, and square foot.

144	square inches make	1	square foot	*ft.*
9	square feet - -	1	square yard	*yd.*
$30\frac{1}{4}$	square yards -	1	square perch	*P.*
40	square perches -	1	rood -	*R.*
4	roods - - -	1	acre -	*A.*

EXAMPLES.

1. Reduce 40 acres to roods. Facit 160 *R.*
2. Reduce 15 roods to square perches. Facit 600 *P.*
3. Bring 28 square perches to square yards. Facit 847 *sq. yd.*
4. Bring 42 square yards to square feet. Facit 378 *sq. ft.*
5. Bring 6 square feet to square inches. Facit 864 *sq. in.*

6. Bring 12 acres to square perches.

Facit 1920 *sq. P.*

LIQUID MEASURE.

This measure is used for beer, cider, wine, &c.

The denominations of Liquid Measure are tun, pipe, or butt, hogshead, gallon, quart, and pint.

2 pints (*pt.*) make	1	quart	*qt.*
4 quarts	1	gallon	*gal.*
63 gallons	1	hogshead	*hhd.*
2 hogsheads	1	pipe or butt	*pi.* or *bt.*
2 pipes (or 4 hogsheads)	1	tun	*T.*

Note.—By a law of Pennsylvania, 16 gallons make one half barrel; $31\frac{1}{2}$ gallons one barrel; 64 gallons one double barrel; 84 gallons one puncheon; 42 gallons one tierce.

EXAMPLES.

1. Reduce 45 tons to pipes. Facit 90 *pi.*
2. Reduce 25 pipes to hogsheads. Facit 50 *hhd.*
3. Bring 9 hogsheads to gallons. Facit 567 *gal.*
4. Bring 40 gallons to quarts. Facit 160 *qt.*
5. Bring 21 quarts to pints. Facit 42 *pt.*
6. Bring 35 gallons to pints. Facit 280 *pt.*
7. Bring 3 tuns to gallons. Facit 756 *gal.*

DRY MEASURE.

This measure is used for grain, fruit, salt, &c.

The denominations of Dry Measure are bushel, peck, quart, and pint.

2 pints (*pt.*) make	1	quart	*qt.*
8 quarts	1	peck	*pe.*
4 pecks	1	bushel	*bu.*

EXAMPLES.

1. Reduce 17 bushels to pecks. Facit 68 *pe.*
2. Reduce 40 pecks to quarts. Facit 320 *qt.*
3. Bring 25 quarts to pints. Facit 50 *pt.*
4. Bring 6 pecks to pints. Facit 96 *pt.*
5. Bring 12 bushels to pints. Facit 768 *pt.*

TIME.

The denominations of Time are year, month, week, day, hour, minute, and second.

60 seconds (*sec.*) make	1	minute	*min.*
60 minutes	1	hour	*H.*
24 hours	1	day	*D.*
7 days	1	week	*W.*
52 weeks, 1 day, and 6 hours, or 365 days, and 6 hours	1	year	*Y.*
12 months (*mo.*)	1	year.	

Note.—The six hours in each year are not reckoned till they amount to one day: hence, a common year consists of 365 days, and every fourth year, called leap year, of 366 days.

The following is a statement of the number of days in each of the twelve months, as they stand in the calendar or almanac:

The fourth, eleventh, ninth, and sixth,
Have thirty days to each affixed;
And every other thirty-one,
Except the second month alone,
Which has but twenty-eight in fine,
Till leap year gives it twenty-nine.

EXAMPLES.

1. Reduce 8 years to months. Facit 96 *mo.*
2. Bring 6 years to weeks (supposing 52 weeks to make a year). Facit 312 *W.*
3. Bring 3 years to days (supposing 365 days to make a year). Facit 1095 *D.*
4. Reduce 25 weeks to days. Facit 175 *D.*
5. Reduce 12 days to hours. Facit 288 *H.*
6. Bring 14 hours to minutes. Facit 840 *min.*
7. Bring 9 minutes to seconds. Facit 540 *sec.*
8. Bring 4 weeks to minutes. Facit 40320 *min.*

When a sum or quantity is to be changed to a higher denomination than its own, work by

RULE 2.*

Divide the given sum or quantity by that number of its own denomination which makes one of the denomi-

* The reason of this rule may be seen by considering that as it takes twenty shillings to make one pound, there must be just as many pounds in any number of shillings as there are twenties in that number; and that to find how many twenties there are in any number, we divide it by 20.

nation to which it is to be changed. (See notes 1, 2, and 3.)

When there are one or more denominations between the denomination of the given sum or quantity and that to which it is to be changed, first change it to the one next higher than its own, and then to the next higher, and so on. (See notes 4 and 5.)

☞ Remainders are of the same denomination as the sum or quantity divided. (See examples 2, 6, 8, 10, and 12, in English Money.)

EXAMPLES.

ENGLISH MONEY.

Note 1.—*To change shillings to pounds, divide them by* 20, *because* 20 *shillings make* 1 *pound.*

1. Bring 60 shillings to pounds. Facit 3£

```
20) 60 (3£          or
    60          2|0) 6|0
    —              ———
                    3£
```

2. Bring 135 shillings to pounds. Facit 6£ 15*s*.

```
20) 135 (6£ 15s.      or
    120           2|0) 13|5
    ———                —
    15s.              6£ 15s.
```

3. Bring 120 shillings to pounds. Facit 6£

4. Bring 446 shillings to pounds. Facit £22 6*s*.

Note 2.—*To bring pence to shillings, divide them by* 12, *because* 12 *pence make* 1 *shilling.*

5. Bring 72 pence to shillings. Facit 6*s*.

6. Bring 195 pence to shillings. Facit 16*s*. 3*d*.

Note 3.—*To bring farthings to pence, divide them by* 4, *because* 4 *farthings make* 1 *penny.*

7. Bring 36 farthings to pence. Facit 9*d*.

8. Bring 763 farthings to pence. Facit 190*d*. 3 *qrs*.

Note 4.—*To bring pence to pounds, bring them first to shillings, and then bring those shillings to pounds.*

9. Bring 480 pence to pounds. Facit 2£

10. Bring 9655 pence to pounds. Facit 40£ 4*s*. 7*d*.

Note 5.—*To bring farthings to pounds, bring them first to pence, then bring those pence to shillings, and then bring those shillings to pounds.*

11. Bring 3840 farthings to pounds. Facit 4£
12. Bring 6529 farthings to pounds.
Facit 6£ 6*s.* 0*d.* $\frac{1}{4}$

FEDERAL MONEY.

Note 6.—*To reduce cents to dollars, divide them by* 100; *or, which is the same thing, separate two figures from the right of their number: and all on the left of these will be dollars.*

1. Bring 600 cents to dollars. Facit 6 dollars.
2. Bring 1250 cents to dollars. Facit 12 dols. 50 cts.
3. Bring 4575 cents to dollars. Facit 45 dols. 75 cts.

Note 7.—*To change fourths of a cent to cents, divide them by* 4—*To change halves of a cent to cents, divide them by* 2—*To change thirds of a cent to cents, divide them by* 3, *&c.*

4. Bring 20 fourths of a cent to cents. Facit 5 cents.
5. Bring 125 fourths of a cent to cents. Facit 31$\frac{1}{4}$ cts.
6. Bring 75 half cents to cents. Facit 37$\frac{1}{2}$ cts.
7. Bring 432 thirds of a cent to cents. Facit 144 cts.

Note 8.—*To change mills to dollars, divide them by* 1000; *or, which is the same thing, separate three figures from the right of their number, and all on the left of these will be dollars.*

8. Bring 4000 mills to dollars. Facit 4 dols.
9. Bring 25750 mills to dollars. Facit 25 dols. 75 cts.
10. Bring 96532 mills to dollars.
Facit 96 dols. 53 cts. 2 m.

AVOIRDUPOIS WEIGHT.

1. Bring 75 cwt. to tons. Facit 3 T. 15 cwt.
2. Bring 56 qrs. to cwt. Facit 14 cwt.
3. Bring 840 lb. to qrs. Facit 30 qrs.
4. Bring 86 oz. to lb. Facit 5 lb. 6 oz.
5. Bring 176 drams to ounces. Facit 11 oz.
6. Bring 958 qr. to tons. Facit 11 T. 19 cwt. 2 qr.
7. Bring 9856 lb. to cwt. Facit 88 cwt.

TROY WEIGHT.

1. Bring 672 oz. to pounds. Facit 56 lb.
2. Bring 145 dwt. to ounces. Facit 7 oz. 5 dwt.
3. Bring 560 gr. to dwt. Facit 23 dwt. 8 gr.
4. Bring 960 dwt. to lb. Facit 4 lb.
5. Bring 9624 gr. to lb. Facit 1 lb. 8 oz. 1 dwt.

APOTHECARIES' WEIGHT.

1. Bring 672 ounces to pounds. Facit 56 ℔
2. Bring 336 drams to ounces. Facit 42 ℥
3. Bring 91 scruples to drams. Facit 30 ʒ 1 ℈
4. Bring 89 grains to ℈. Facit 4 ℈ 9 grs.
5. Bring 192 ℈ to ℥. Facit 8 ℥
6. Bring 12660 gr. to ℔. Facit 2 ℔ to 2 ℥ 3 ʒ.

LONG MEASURE.

1. Bring 60 miles to leagues. Facit 20 L.
2. Bring 567 furlongs to miles. Facit 70 M. 7 fur.
3. Bring 640 poles to furlongs. Facit 16 fur.
4. Bring 286 yards to poles. Facit 52 P.
5. Bring 52 feet to yards. Facit 17 yds. 1 ft.
6. Bring 588 inches to feet. Facit 49 ft.
7. Bring 2880 poles to leagues. Facit 3 L.
8. Bring 75 inches to yards. Facit 2 yds. 0 ft. 3 in.

CLOTH MEASURE.

1. Bring 60 qr. to French ells. Facit 10 E. Fr.
2. Bring 464 qrs. to English ells. Facit 92 E. E. 4 qr.
3. Bring 750 qrs. to Flemish ells. Facit 250 E. Fl.
4. Bring 46 qrs. to yards. Facit 11 yds. 2 qrs.
5. Bring 480 nails to quarters. Facit 120 qr.
6. Bring 95 nails to English ells. Facit 4 E.E. 3qr. 3na.

LAND MEASURE.

1. Bring 286 roods to acres. Facit 71 A. 2 R.
2. Bring 360 square perches to roods. Facit 9 R.
3. Bring 4719 square yards to square perches. Facit 156 P.
4. Bring 756 square feet to square yards. Facit 84 yds.
5. Bring 1728 square inches to square feet. Facit 12 ft.
6. Bring 966 square perches to acres. Facit 6 A. 0 R. 6 P.

LIQUID MEASURE.

1. Bring 91 pipes to tuns. Facit 45 T. 1 P.
2. Bring 50 hogsheads to pipes. Facit 25 pi.
3. Bring 945 gallons to hogsheads. Facit 15 hhd.
4. Bring 163 quarts to gallons. Facit 40 gal. 3 qt.
5. Bring 87 pints to quarts. Facit 43 qt. 1 pt.

6. Bring 59 hhd. to tuns. Facit 14 T. 3 hhd.
7. Bring 6048 pints to tuns. Facit 3 T.

DRY MEASURE.

1. Bring 308 pecks to bushels. Facit 77 bu.
2. Bring 246 quarts to pecks. Facit 30 pe. 6 qt.
3. Bring 300 pints to quarts. Facit 150 qt.
4. Bring 486 quarts to bushels. Facit 15 bu. 0 pe. 6 qt.
5. Bring 384 pints to bushels. Facit 6 bu.

TIME.

1. Bring 675 months to years. Facit 56 Y. 3 mo.
2. Bring 208 weeks to years (supposing 52 weeks to make a year). Facit 4 Y.
3. Bring 4386 days to years (supposing 365 days to make a year). Facit 12 Y. 6 D.
4. Bring 72 days to weeks. Facit 10 W. 2 D.
5. Bring 4440 hours to days. Facit 185 D.
6. Bring 726 minutes to hours. Facit 12 h. 6 min.
7. Bring 360 seconds to minutes. Facit 6 min.
8. Bring 30240 minutes to weeks. Facit 3 W.

PROMISCUOUS EXAMPLES.

1. How many shillings are there in 20 pounds? Ans. 400.
2. What number of pounds do 65 shillings make? Ans. 3£ 5*s*.
3. How many cents are there in 65 dollars? Ans. 6500.
4. In 3400 cents, how many dollars? Ans. 34.
5. How many quarters of a cent are there in 96 cents? Ans. 384.
6. How many cents are there in 480 quarters of a cent? Ans. 120.
7. What number of half pence do 45 pence make? Ans. 90.
8. How many three pences are there in 10 shillings? Ans. 40.
9. How many six pences are there in 6 shillings? Ans. 12.
10. How many shillings are there in 18 three pences? Ans. 4*s*. 6*d*.

11. How many pennyweights are there in 50 grains? (Troy Weight.) Ans. 2 dwt. 2 gr.

12. How many ounces are there in 15 pounds? (Troy Weignt.) Ans. 180.

13. In 86 drams, how many ounces? (Avoir. Wt.) Ans. 5 oz. 6 dr.

14. In 5 tons, how many hundred weight? (Avoir. Weight.) Ans. 100.

15. How many scruples are there in 15 drams? Ans. 5.

16. How many ounces are there in 14 pounds? (Apoth. Weight.) Ans. 168.

17. How many inches are there in 12 feet? Ans. 144.

18. In 25 furlongs, how many miles? Ans. 3 m. 1 fur.

19. How many nails are there in 3 quarters of a yard? Ans. 12.

20. How many English ells are there in 75 quarters of a yard? Ans. 15.

21. How many square yards are there in 37 square feet? Ans. 4 yd. 1 ft.

22. In 125 roods, how many square perches? Ans. 5000.

23. In 79 pints, how many quarts? Ans. 39 qt. 1 pt.

24. How many gallons are there in three hogsheads? Ans. 189.

25. In 900 pecks, how many bushels? Ans. 225.

26. How many minutes are there in 360 seconds? Ans. 6.

27. How many days are there in 12 weeks? Ans. 84.

COMPOUND ADDITION.

Compound Addition is the adding of sums or quantities which consist of several denominations.

RULE.

Place the sums or quantities so that the numbers of the same denomination may stand directly under each other, and form a separate column; then add up the severa. columns, successively, beginning with the one of the lowest denomination: if the amount of either of the columns be not as much as 1 of the next higher denomination, set it down; but if it be, reduce it to that denomination, and add the number it contains of said denomination into the column of the same.

If a remainder occur on reducing the amount of any column, set it under that column.

Proof: as in Simple Addition.

MONEY.

PENCE TABLE.			TABLE OF SHILLINGS.		
d.	*s.*	*d.*	*s.*	£	*s.*
20 pence make -	1	8	20 - - -	1	0
30 - - -	2	6	30 - - -	1	10
40 - - -	3	4	40 - - -	2	0
50 - - -	4	2	50 - - -	2	10
60 - - -	5	0	60 - - -	3	0
70 - - -	5	10	70 - - -	3	10
80 - - -	6	8	80 - - -	4	0
90 - - -	7	6	90 - - -	4	10
100 - - -	8	4	100 - - -	5	0
110 - - -	9	2	110 - - -	5	10
120 - - -	10	0	120 - - -	6	0
240 - - -	20	0	130 - - -	6	10

EXAMPLES.

£	s.	d.	£	s.	d.	£	s.	d.
10	2	3	175	12	6	456	12	$5\frac{1}{2}$
45	10	2	280	10	4	320	12	0
36	1	1	362	8	3	400	10	$1\frac{3}{4}$
20	3	0	484	13	10	45	6	$2\frac{1}{4}$
120	0	5	40	18	11	1000	18	$3\frac{1}{4}$
231	16	11	1344	3	10	2223	19	$0\frac{3}{4}$

£	s.	d.	£	s.	d.	£	s.	d.	£	s.	d.
75	10	2	14	0	0	12	2	0	25	0	6
13	3	0	24	10	6	10	0	0	14	6	8
5	3	0	36	4	8	15	3	6	17	10	9
4	2	1	45	0	11	4	5	0	18	0	0
6	1	8	14	0	0	2	7	6	20	0	0

£	s.	d.	£	s.	d.	£	s.	d.
174	14	10½	4900	16	10½	340	0	0
240	18	7	3704	0	3¾	222	0	0
320	14	8¼	2000	0	0	1346	18	0
642	7	2½	4540	10	2¼	2432	2	3
438	14	10¾	3200	15	0½	3460	15	9½
346	3	5½	4620	18	4	3420	10	2¾

11. Add the following sums: viz. 15£ 6s. 3d.—75£ 10s. 2d.—65£ and 94£.

12. Add 45£ 12s. 3d.—56£ 10s.—346£ 18s.—and 1£ 19s. 2¼d.

13. Add 145£—72£ 0s. 3d.—14£ 8s. 9½d.—18s. 9¾d.—and 42£ 2s. 4¾d.

14. Add 410£ 5s.—1600£ 18s.—and 4426£ 19s.

TROY WEIGHT.

lb.	*oz.*	*lb.*	*oz.*	*dwt.*	*lb.*	*oz.*	*dwt.*	*gr.*
37	11	93	11	18	17	9	11	15
62	0	6	0	1	82	2	0	0
72	10	14	4	12	12	8	16	0
13	4	72	11	3	9	4	0	0

4. Add 2*lb.* 11*oz.* 10*dwt.* 2*gr.*—15*lb.* 10*oz.* 2 *dwt.*—and 145*lb.* 2 *oz.* 2 *dwt.*

5. Add 14*lb.* 2*oz.*—2*lb.* 0*oz.* 10*dwt.*—15*lb.* 5*oz.* 19*dwt.* 14*gr.*—and 25*lb.* 10*oz.*

AVOIRDUPOIS WEIGHT.

T.	*cwt.*	*qrs.*	*T.*	*cwt.*	*qrs.*	*lb.*	*cwt.*	*qr.*	*lb.*	*oz.*	*dr.*
40	11	3	3	19	3	27	8	3	12	15	8
15	10	2	2	12	1	12	12	0	2	9	4
18	0	1	10	5	0	0	8	2	1	0	3
9	12	0		3	2	10	9	1	26	8	2

4. Add 20 tons, two hundred weight, 2 quarters; 12 tons; 15 tons, 2 quarters; and 2 tons.

5. Add 15 hundred weight, 3 quarters, 27 pounds;

17 hundred weight, 15 pounds; and 1 hundred weight, 10 pounds.

APOTHECARIES' WEIGHT.

℔	℥	ʒ
7	3	2
4	2	1
8	0	4
2	9	0

℔	℥	ʒ	℈
10	4	0	2
12	7	4	0
9	6	3	1
4	0	7	1

℔	℥	ʒ	℈	*gr.*
4	3	2	1	0
14	11	7	2	0
		1	1	2
			2	1

4. Add 10 pounds, 7 drams, 2 scruples; 15 pounds, 11 ounces, 2 drams; 45 pounds, 4 ounces; and 36 pounds.

5. Add 14 pounds, 2 ounces; 1 pound, 3 grains; 2 ounces, 3 drams, 2 scruples; and 4 drams, 12 grains.

LONG MEASURE.

L.	*M.*	*F.*
7	2	7
6	1	4
12	1	0
14	0	3

L.	*M.*	*F.*	*P.*
8	2	7	16
20	2	7	1
24	1	4	9
50	0	0	0

yd.	*ft.*	*in.*
2	2	9
1	1	0
10	1	3
12	0	4

4. Add 14 leagues, 2 miles, 6 furlongs; 4 leagues, 4 furlongs, 30 poles; 1 league, 2 miles, 15 poles; and 42 leagues.

5. Add 2 yards, 2 feet, 9 inches; 1 yard, 11 inches; 1 foot, 6 inches; and 10 yards, 5 inches.

CLOTH MEASURE.

yd.	*qr.*	*na.*
79	2	1
25	1	3
14	3	2
46	2	1

E.E.	*qr.*	*na.*
86	4	2
44	3	0
21	0	2
5	0	3

E.Fl.	*qr.*	*na.*
14	2	1
25	1	0
14	0	3
25	0	0

4. Add 15 yards, 3 quarters, 2 nails; 45 yards, 2 quarters; 1 yard, 3 nails; and 125 yards.

5. Add 14 English ells, 3 quarters; 25 English ells, 2 quarters, 3 nails; and 3 quarters, 1 nail.

LAND MEASURE.

A.	*R.*	*P.*		*A.*	*R.*	*P.*		*yd.*	*ft.*	*in.*
75	3	2		150	3	39		8	2	12
24	0	0		265	2	11		10	1	95
98	1	0		284	1	9		12	1	115
75	3	0		326	0	0		20	0	46

4. Add 125 acres, 2 roods; 400 acres, 3 roods, 28 perches; 56 acres, 20 perches; and 500 acres.

5. Add 15 yards, 2 feet; 2 yards, 1 foot; 14 yards, 2 feet; and 25 yards.

LIQUID MEASURE.

T.	*hhd.*	*gal.*		*hhd.*	*gal.*	*qt.*		*gal.*	*qt.*	*pt.*
12	2	45		2	15	3		24	2	1
10	1	17		4	14	2		14	1	0
24	0	0		10	6	2		6	3	0
20	3	0		12	0	0		8	2	1

4. Add 10 tuns, 3 hogsheads, 15 gallons; 4 tons, 2 hogsheads, 9 gallons; 2 hogsheads, 46 gallons; and 14 tuns.

5. Add 14 gallons, 3 quarts, 1 pint; 25 gallons, 2 quarts; 2 gallons, 2 pints; and 13 gallons.

DRY MEASURE.

bu.	*pe.*	*qt.*		*bu.*	*pe.*	*qt.*		*bu.*	*pe.*	*qt.*	*pt.*
25	3	2		10	3	2		36	1	1	1
18	2	0		117	1	3		48	3	2	1
21	1	0		215	2	4		50	0	0	0
40	0	0		450	3	0			3	7	1

4. Add 115 bushels, 3 pecks, 7 quarts; 345 bushels, 2 pecks; 40 bushels, 4 quarts; and 375 bushels.

5. Add 2 bushels, 3 pecks, 4 quarts, 1 pint; 4 bushels, 2 pecks, 2 quarts; and 1 peck, 6 quarts, 1 pint.

TIME.

Y	*mo.*
75	5
16	10
14	11
25	2

W.	*D.*	*H.*	*min.*
2	1	10	40
1	6	9	20
3	5	20	12
2	3	7	56

D.	*H.*	*min*	*sec.*
4	20	56	54
3	19	25	22
2	8	0	3
	6	0	0

4. Add 10 years, 3 months; 45 years, 6 months; 75 years, 11 months; 15 years; and 96 years.

5. Add 7 weeks, 1 day, 5 hours, 45 minutes; 2 weeks, 4 days, 22 hours; 6 days, 15 hours, 10 minutes; and 5 hours.

APPLICATION.

1. Bought an English Reader, for 5s. 7½d.; a Sequel, for 6s. 6½d.; an Arithmetic, for 3s. 9d.; and a Slate for 2s. 4d. What do they all come to? Ans. 18s. 3d.

2. If a storekeeper buy cloth to the amount of 310£ 7s. 6d.; linen to the amount of 37£ 5s.; and groceries to the amount of 209£ 15s. 4½d.: what sum must he pay for the whole? Ans. 557£ 7s. 10½d.

3. Bought a horse for 17£ 10s. 6d.; a cow for 5£ 14s. 7d.; and a quantity of hay for 6£ 12s. 6d. What is the amount? Ans. 29£ 17s. 7d.

4. Laid out in market, for a pair of fowls, 5s. 7½d.; for a goose, 7s. 6d.; for a bushel of potatoes, 3s. 9d.; for a piece of beef, 15s.; and for turnips, 4s. 8d. How much was laid out in all? Ans. 1£ 16s. 6½d.

5. Bought of a silversmith, dishes, weighing 16lb. 10oz. 13dwt.; plates, weighing 35lb. 10oz. 11dwt.; tablespoons, 6lb. 11oz.; and tea-spoons, 2lb. 8oz. What was the weight of the whole? Ans. 62lb. 4oz. 4dwt.

6. A grocer bought four hogsheads of sugar, which weighed as follows—No. 1, 8cwt. 1 qr. 26lb.; No. 2, 9cwt. 3qrs. 11lb.; No. 3, 12 cwt. 2 qrs. 19 lb.; No. 4, 12cwt. 2qrs. What did the whole weigh?
Ans. 43cwt. 2qrs.

7. Sold three boxes of spice weighing as follows—No. 1, 1qr. 12lb. 9oz. 14dr.; No. 2, 2qrs. 13lb. 15oz. 8dr.; No. 3, 1qr. 25lb. 13oz. 12dr. How much was the whole weight? Ans. 1cwt. 1qr. 24lb. 7oz. 2dr.

8. If a druggist mix several simples together, the first, 4 ounces, 3 drams, 2 scruples; the second, 3 ounces, 1 dram, 1 scruple, 17 grains; the third, 1 pound, 7 ounces, 3 drams, 1 scruple: what will be the weight of the mixture? Ans. 2℔ 3℥ 0ʒ 1℈ 17gr.

9. Admit a man travelled in one day, 27 miles, 2 furlongs; in another, 32 miles, 7 furlongs, 33 perches; in another, 19 miles, 7 furlongs, 16 perches; and in another, 12 miles, 5 furlongs: how far did he travel in all? Ans. 92m. 6fur. 9P.

10. There are three pieces of silver wire: the first measures 10 yards, 2 feet, 6 inches; the second, 15 yards, 1 foot, 4 inches; the third, 20 yards, 11 inches: what is the length of the whole? Ans. 46yds. 1ft. 9in.

11. There are four pieces of linen: the first contains 27 yards, 2 quarters; the second, 41 yards, 3 quarters; the third, 36 yards, 1 quarter; and the fourth, 33 yards, 2 quarters. How many yards are there in the four pieces? Ans. 139yds.

12. Bought three pieces of lace containing as follows —No. 1, 17 yards, 3 quarters, 2 nails; No. 2, 25 yards, 2 quarters, 1 nail; No. 3, 32 yards, 3 quarters, 3 nails. How many yards were bought in all?
Ans. 76yds. 1qr. 2na.

13. A person has three farms: the first contains 120 acres, 3 roods; the second, 256 acres, 1 rood; and the third, 300 acres. How many acres in all? Ans. 677.

14. Sold two casks of cider, one of which contained 31 gallons, 3 quarts, and the other 36 gallons, 2 quarts, 1 pint. How much was there in the two? Ans. 68 gals. 1qt. 1pt.

15. There are three bags of wheat: the first contains 2 bushels, 3 pecks, 7 quarts; the second, 3 bushels, 3 pecks, 4 quarts; the third, 4 bushels. How much is in the three bags? Ans. 10bu. 3pe. 3qt.

16 Bought 136 bushels of corn of one man; 197 bushels, 2 pecks, of another; 200 bushels, 1 peck, 6 quarts, of a third; and 764 bushels, 3 pecks, 7 quarts, of a fourth. How much was bought in all?
Ans. 1298bu. 3pe. 5qt.

17. A person who was born in Philadelphia, resided in that place till he was 21 years, 3 weeks old. He then went to Wilmington, spending 2 days on the road.

He resided in Wilmington 5 years, and at the end of that time removed to Baltimore; the journey occupying 3 days. He remained in Baltimore 2 years, 3 weeks, and 3 days, and then removed to Richmond, being 5 days in travelling thither. What was his age at the time he arrived in Richmond?

Ans. 28 years, 7 weeks, and 6 days.

COMPOUND SUBTRACTION.

Compound subtraction teaches to find the difference between any two sums or quantities, which consist of several denominations.

RULE.

Place the sums or quantities as in Compound Addition, with the less under the greater; then, beginning with the lowest denomination, subtract each under number from the one above it, and set down the remainder: but if the number of either denomination in the under sum be greater than the one above it, subtract it from as many of that denomination as will make one of the next higher, add the difference to the upper number, set down the amount, and carry 1 to the under number of the next higher denomination.

Proof: as in Simple Subtraction.

EXAMPLES.

MONEY.

	£	s.	d.	£	s.	d.	£	s.	d.
From	5	0	6	10	6	3	145	18	9½
Take	2	9	3	5	7	6	104	12	10¼
Rem.	2	11	3	4	18	9	41	5	11¼

£	s.	d.	£	s.	d.	£	s.	d.	£	s.	d.
5	10	3	37	12	6	25	4	9	46	2	3
4	6	2	27	18	9	14	5	6	25	1	9

£	s.	d.	£	s.	d.	£	s.	d.
45	6	$3\frac{3}{4}$	142	10	$3\frac{1}{2}$	2640	18	$11\frac{1}{4}$
22	4	$6\frac{1}{2}$	45	9	$2\frac{3}{4}$	1221	19	$6\frac{1}{2}$

11. Subtrac. 24 pounds, 10 shillings, and 6 pence, from 36 pounds, 9 shillings, and 3 pence.

12. Subtract 26 pounds, from 120 pounds, 15 shillings, and 9 pence.

13. Subtract 9000 pounds, from 9672 pounds, 18 shillings, and $11\frac{1}{2}$ pence.

14. Subtract 45 pounds, 14 shillings, and $3\frac{1}{2}$ pence, from 500 pounds.

TROY WEIGHT.

	lb.	*oz.*	*lb.*	*oz.*	*dwt.*	*lb.*	*oz.*	*dwt.*	*gr.*
From	48	2	15	5	2	45	9	4	3
Take	10	1	12	0	2	15	6	18	17
Rem.									

4. Subtract 14 pounds, 9 ounces, from 65 pounds, 3 ounces, 10 pennyweights.

5. Subtract 10 pounds, 6 ounces, 10 pennyweights, 11 grains, from 15 pounds, 6 grains.

AVOIRDUPOIS WEIGHT.

	T.	*cwt.*	*qr.*	*T.*	*cwt.*	*qr.*	*lb.*	*cwt.*	*qr.*	*lb.*	*oz.*	*dr.*
From	45	11	3	52	12	3	15	17	0	0	0	0
Take	15	10	2	24	10	0	26	6	3	21	15	9
Rem.												

4. Subtract 76 tons, 18 hundred weight, 3 quarters, from 195 tons, 2 hundred weight, 2 quarters.

5. Subtract 14 pounds, 6 ounces, 3 drams, from 20 pounds, 2 ounces.

APOTHECARIES' WEIGHT.

	℔	℥	ʒ	℔	℥	ʒ	℈	℔	℥	ʒ	℈	*gr.*
From	48	2	2	22	0	1	0	42	2	2	0	1
Take	10	1	2	12	3	2	1	25	0	0	0	3
Rem.												

4. Subtract 16 pounds, 5 ounces, 2 drams, from 24 pounds, 10 ounces, 3 drams.

5. Take 3 ounces, 3 drams, 2 scruples, from 5 pounds, 9 ounces, 2 drams, 2 grains.

LONG MEASURE.

	L.	*M*	*fur.*	*L.*	*M.*	*fur.*	*P.*	*yds.*	*ft.*	*in.*
From	24	1	7	56	1	0	19	6	2	10
Take	18	2	4	10	0	7	20	3	2	7
Rem.										

4. Subtract 45 miles, 5 furlongs, 20 poles, from 320 miles, 3 furlongs, 36 poles.

5. Subtract 15 yards, 2 feet, 6 inches, from 36 yards, 1 foot, 11 inches.

CLOTH MEASURE.

	yds.	*qrs.*	*na.*	*E. E.*	*qrs.*	*na.*	*E. Fl.*	*qrs.*	*na.*
From	71	3	1	42	0	2	51	2	2
Take	14	2	3	19	2	3	42	2	1
Rem.									

4. Subtract 95 yards, 3 quarters, 2 nails, from 156 yards, 2 quarters, 3 nails.

5. Subtract 14 English ells, 1 quarter, 2 nails, from 52 English ells, 3 quarters, 2 nails.

LAND MEASURE.

	A.	*R.*	*P.*	*A.*	*R.*	*P.*	*yds.*	*ft.*	*in.*
From	96	3	36	195	2	2	25	2	72
Take	25	2	39	36	3	1	14	7	10
Rem.									

4. Subtract 36 acres, 2 roods, from 900 acres, 3 roods, 16 perches.

5. Subtract 72 acres, from 360 acres, 2 roods, 29 perches.

LIQUID MEASURE.

	Tun.	hhd.	gal.	hhd.	gal.	qt.	gal.	qt.	pt.
From	25	3	45	45	13	2	75	3	1
Take	17	2	62	25	2	3	22	1	0
Rem.									

4. Subtract 14 tuns, 2 hogsheads, 10 gallons, from 24 tuns, 1 hogshead, 9 gallons.

5. Take 22 hogsheads, 2 quarts, from 95 hogsheads, 10 gallons, 3 quarts, 1 pint.

DRY MEASURE.

	bu.	pe.	qt.	bu.	pe.	qt.	pe.	qt.	pt.
From	95	3	2	84	2	1	3	7	0
Take	22	0	1	36	3	2	2	3	1
Rem.									

4. Subtract 125 bushels, 3 pecks, 2 quarts, from 195 bushels.

5. Subtract 450 bushels, from 500 bushels, 3 pecks.

TIME.

	Y.	mo.	W.	D.	H.	D.	H.	min.	sec.
From	75	3	32	6	20	36	14	30	25
Take	25	4	12	4	22	15	12	25	32
Rem.									

4. Subtract 125 years, 9 months, from 450 years, 11 months.

5. Take 122 days, 18 hours, 36 minutes, from 200 days, 18 hours.

APPLICATION.

1. A merchant has in his desk 375£ 10s. If he take out 122£ 11s. 3d. to pay for goods, how much will remain? Ans. 252£ 18s. 9d.

2. A person borrowed of me 125£ 10s. 6d., but has since paid me 75£ 18s. 2d. How much does he still owe me? Ans. 49£ 12s. 4d.

3. If a merchant buy a quantity of tobacco, for 1500 pounds, 16 shillings, and afterwards sell it for 1595 pounds, 19 shillings, and 9 pence; how much will he gain by the transaction? Ans. 95£ 3s. 9d.

4. If a person sell goods for 136 pounds, 12 shillings, and 6 pence, which cost him 149 pounds, 10 shillings, and 3 pence, how much will he lose by the sale?
Ans. 12£ 17s. 9d.

5. A silversmith had 26 pounds, 9 ounces, 10 pennyweights of silver, but sold 18 pounds, 16 pennyweights, 10 grains. How much had he left?
Ans. 8 lb. 8 oz. 13 dwt. 14 gr.

6. A grocer has 13 hundred weight, 2 quarters, 16 pounds of sugar. If he sell 9 hundred weight, 2 quarters, 7 pounds, how much will remain unsold?
Ans. 4 cwt. 9 lb.

7. There is a quantity of spice, which, with the box that contains it, weighs 34 pounds, 10 ounces, 1 dram; the box itself weighs 10 pounds, 10 ounces, 2 drams. What is the weight of the spice? Ans. 23 lb. 15 oz. 15 dr.

8. If out of 6 pounds, 10 ounces, 6 drams, 2 scruples of medicine, be taken 4 pounds, 5 ounces, 4 drams, 1 scruple, 17 grains; what quantity will remain?
Ans. 2℔ 5℥ 2ʒ 0℈ 3 grs.

9. A certain rope is 365 yards, 1 foot, 6 inches long. If 84 yards, 2 feet, 4 inches, be cut off from it, how long will the remainder be? Ans. 280 yds. 2 ft. 2 in.

10. The distance from Philadelphia to Trenton is about 30 miles, 3 furlongs, 16 poles. A person, going from one place to the other, stopped at an inn, when he had travelled 18 miles, 3 furlongs, 26 poles. How much further had he still to go? Ans. 11 M. 7 fur. 30 P.

11. Bought 145 yards, 3 quarters, of cloth, and sold thereof 95 yards, 2 quarters, 3 nails. How much remains? Ans. 50 yds. 1 na.

12. If from a piece of cambric, containing 25 yards, 3 quarters, 3 nails, there be taken 16 yards, 2 quarters, how much will be left? Ans. 9 yds. 1 qr. 3 na.

13. A farmer had 450 acres, 3 roods of land, but gave his son 150 acres, 3 roods, 25 perches. How much had he remaining? Ans. 299 A. 3 R. 15 P.

14. Bought several casks of cider, containing in all,

120 gallons, 3 quarts; and disposed of one cask which contained 31 gallons, 2 quarts, 1 pint. How much is there in the other casks? Ans. 89 gal. 1 pt.

15. From a barrel of beer containing 31 gallons, 2 qts., there has been drawn 15 gallons, 2 quarts, 1 pint. How much remains in the barrel? Ans. 15 gal. 3 qt. 1 pt.

16. Out of a granary which contained 500 bushels of wheat, there has been taken 374 bushels, 2 pecks, 7 quarts. What quantity remains? Ans. 125 bu. 1 pe. 1 qt.

17. Charles was bound as an apprentice for 7 years. He has served 2 years, and 5 months. How long has he still to serve? Ans. 4 Y. 7 mo.

18. James is 13 years, 2 months old, and John 9 years, 3 months. How much older is James than John?

Ans. 3 Y. 11 mo.

Note.—The interval or space of time between two given dates is thus found:—Set the prior date under the subsequent date; and when the lower number of days is greater than the upper, take it from as many days as are in the month of the prior date, add the difference to the upper number, and set down the amount; then carry one to the months of the prior date, and subtract as in the foregoing examples.

19. Henry was born on the 20th of the 8th month, 1789, and Charles on the 18th of the 9th month, 1808. What is the difference in their ages?

	Y.	*mo.*	*da.*	
	1808	9	18	subsequent date.
	1789	8	20	prior date.
Ans.	19	0	29	

20. A person was born on the 18th of the 5th month, (May,) 1781. What was his age on the 12th of the 7th month, (July,) 1808. Ans. 27 Y. 1 mo. 25 D.

21. A bond was given the 21st of the 11th month, (November,) 1798, and was taken up the 12th of the 9th month, (September,) 1811. What time elapsed from the day the bond was given till the day it was taken up?

Ans. 12 Y. 9 mo. 21 D.

COMPOUND MULTIPLICATION.

Compound Multiplication is the multiplying of any sum or quantity which consists of divers denominations.

When the multiplier does not exceed 12, work by

RULE I.

Multiply the several denominations of the given sum or quantity, one after another, beginning with the lowest: if the product of either of them be not equal to one or more of the next higher denomination, set it down: but if it be, reduce it to that denomination, and add the number it contains thereof to the product of the same; and so proceed. If, on reducing the product of any denomination, there be a remainder, it must be placed under that denomination.

PROOF.

Double the multiplicand, and multiply by half the multiplier.

EXAMPLES.

MONEY.

£ s. d.	£ s. d.	£ s. d.	£ s. d.
5 4 2	10 15 6	21 9 $2\frac{1}{4}$	15 0 $9\frac{3}{4}$
2	3	4	5
10 8 4	32 6 6	85 16 9	75 4 $0\frac{3}{4}$

£ s. d.	£ s. d.	£ s. d.	£ s. d.
4 2 1	12 3 9	25 4 $1\frac{1}{2}$	96 4 $9\frac{1}{4}$
3	6	7	8

		£ s. d.				£ s. d.
9.	Multiply	2 6 4	by 5		Product	11 11 8
10.	———	16 $3\frac{1}{4}$	by 6		———	4 17 $7\frac{1}{2}$
11.	———	1 2 $6\frac{1}{4}$	by 9		———	10 2 $8\frac{1}{4}$
12.	———	1 3 2	by 10		———	11 11 8
13.	———	12 $9\frac{1}{2}$	by 11		———	7 0 $8\frac{1}{2}$
14.	———	1 2 $1\frac{1}{4}$	by 12		———	13 5 3

WEIGHTS AND MEASURES.

lb.	*oz.*	*dwt.*	*gr.*
17	10	12	6
			3

T.	*cwt.*	*qrs.*	*lb.*	*oz.*	*dr.*
6	17	3	13	2	15
					4

℔	℥	ʒ	℈	*gr.*
4	10	7	2	13
				5

L.	*M.*	*fur.*	*P.*
15	2	7	30
			6

yds.	*ft.*	*in.*
14	2	11
		7

yds.	*qrs.*	*na.*
16	3	3
		8

E.E.	*qrs.*	*na.*
12	4	1
		9

A.	*R.*	*P.*
47	3	15
		2

T.	*hhd.*	*gal.*	*qt.*	*pt.*
2	3	40	3	1
				10

bu.	*pe.*	*qt.*
6	3	7
		5

bu.	*pe.*	*qt.*
14	3	2
		6

W.	*D.*	*H.*	*min.*	*sec.*
4	5	20	32	10
				7

When the multiplier exceeds 12, and is the product of two factors in the multiplication table, work by

RULE 2.

Multiply the given sum by one of said factors, and then multiply the product by the other factor.

Proof: Change the factors.

EXAMPLES.

1. Multiply £3 2*s.* $6\frac{1}{2}$*d.* by 14. Product £43 15*s.* 7*d.*

	£	*s.*	*d.*
	3	2	$6\frac{1}{2}$
			2
	6	5	1
			7
Product	43	15	7

	£	*s.*	*d.*
	3	2	$6\frac{1}{2}$
			7
	21	17	$9\frac{1}{2}$
			2
Proof	43	15	7

	£	s.	d.				£	s.	d.
2. Multiply	1	12	3	by	15	Product	24	3	9
3. ———	2	14	1½	by	54	———	146	2	9
4 ———		11	1¼	by	96	———	53	6	0
5. ———		12	3¼	by	35	———	21	9	5¾
6. ———		7	6	by	120	———	45	0	0

When the multiplier is not the exact product of any two factors in the multiplication table, work by

RULE 3.

Use those two factors whose product is the least short of the multiplier; then multiply the given sum by the number which supplies the deficiency, and add its product to the sum produced by the two factors.

EXAMPLES.

1. Multiply 2£ 1*s.* 3*d.* by 68. Product 140£ 5*s.*

	£	s.	d.			£	s.	d.	
	2	1	3	×2		2	1	3	×2
			11					6	
	22	13	9			12	7	6	
			6					11	
	136	2	6			136	2	6	
	4	2	6			4	2	6	
Prod.	140	5	0		Proof	140	5	0	

	£	s.	d.				£	s.	d.
2. Multiply	3	13	4	by	31	Product	113	13	4
3. ———	1	18	10	by	68	———	132	0	8
4. ———	1	11	6	by	23	———	36	4	6
5. ———		16	6½	by	47	———	38	17	5½
6. ———		16	8	by	112	———	93	6	8

When the multiplier is greater than the product of any two factors in the multiplication table, work by

RULE 4.

Multiply continually by as many tens less one, as there are figures in the multiplier; then multiply the last product by the left hand figure of the multiplier, (if greater than 1;) again, multiply the given sum by the units figure of the multiplier,—the product of the first ten by the tens figure,—the product of the second ten (if any) by the hundreds figure, &c.; then add the products of these several figures together, and their amount will be the product required.

EXAMPLES.

1. Multiply 1 s. 7½ d. by 276.

	s.	d.	
	1	7½	×6
		10	
	16	3	×7
		10	
8	2	6	
		2	
16	5	0	
	9	9	
5	13	9	
Prod. 22	8	6	

2. Multiply 2 s. 6 d. by 3452

		s.	d.	
		2	6	×2
			10	
	1	5	0	×5
			10	
	12	10	0	×4
			10	
	125	0	0	
			3	
	375	0	0	
		5	0	
	6	5	0	
	50	0	0	
Prod.	431	10	0	

	£	s.	d.				£	s.	d.
3. Multiply		1	2	by	195	Product	11	7	6
4. ———		1	3	by	435	———	27	3	9
5. ———		3	3	by	407	———	66	2	9
6. ———		2	4	by	820	———	95	13	4
7. ———	1	3	6	by	165	———	193	17	6
8. ———			6½	by	276	———	7	9	6
9. ———			11¼	by	2123	———	99	10	3¾

APPLICATION.

1. If one pound of sugar cost 1 s. 1 d., what will 4 pounds cost? Ans. 4 s. 4 d.

2. If one yard of muslin cost 9 s. 4½ d., what is the price of 7 yards? Ans. 3 L. 5 s. 7½ d

3. What will 5 yards of broad cloth come to, at 2 L. 5 s. per yard? Ans. 11 L. 5 s.

4. What will 9 hundred weight of flour amount to, at 1 L. 11 s. 5 d. a hundred weight? Ans. 14 L. 2 s. 9 d.

5. Sold 10 tons of hay, at 8 L. 12 s. 6½ d. a ton, what is the amount? Ans. 86 L. 5 s. 5 d.

6. How much will 66 acres of land come to, at 7 L. 9 s. 6 d. an acre? Ans. 493 L. 7 s.

7. What will 32 pounds of cheese cost, at 3 s. 11 d. a pound? Ans. 6 L. 5 s. 4 d.

8. Bought 63 gallons of wine, at 5 s. 4 d. per gallon, what was the amount? Ans. 16 L. 16 s.

9. What is the value of 336 yards of linen, at 2 s. 5 d. per yard? Ans. 40 L. 12 s.

10. How much will 240 bushels of wheat come to, at 14 s. 6 d. per bushel? Ans. 174 L.

11. If one pound of sugar cost 1 s. 1½ d., what will 109 pounds come to? Ans. 6 L. 2 s. 7½ d.

12. What will 400 pounds of lead come to, at 8½ d. per pound? Ans. 14 L. 3 s. 4 d.

13. How much will 1500 gallons of oil amount to, at 6 s. 2 d. per gallon? Ans. 462 L. 10 s.

14. A goldsmith bought 11 ingots of silver, each of which weighed 4 pounds, 1 ounce, 15 pennyweights, 22 grains. What is the weight of the whole?
Ans. 45 lb. 7 oz. 15 dwt. 2 gr.

15. A grocer bought 5 hogsheads of sugar, weighing each 12 cwt. 1 qr. 27 lb. How much did the whole weigh? Ans. 62 cwt. 1 qr. 23 lb.

16. Sold 10 pieces of cloth, measuring each 17 yards, 3 quarters, 2 nails. How many yards were there in all?
Ans. 178 yds. 3 qrs.

17. There are 5 bags of apples, each of which contains 2 bushels, 3 pecks. How many bushels are there in the whole? Ans. 13 bu. 3 pe.

COMPOUND DIVISION.

Compound Division teaches to divide any sum or quantity which consists of several denominations.

When the divisor does not exceed 12, work by

RULE 1.

Divide the several denominations of the given sum

or quantity, one after another, (beginning with the highest,) and set their respective quotients underneath. When a remainder occurs, reduce it to the next lower denomination, and add it to that denomination in the given sum or quantity.

If the number of either denomination be not large enough to contain the divisor, reduce it to the next lower denomination, and add it thereto; then divide as before.

PROOF.

Multiply the quotient by the divisor, and the product will be equal to the dividend.

EXAMPLES.

£ s. d.	£ s. d.	£ s. d.	£ s. d.
2)6 6 4	4)10 7 4	8)20 2 0	6)5 2 9
3 3 2	2 11 10	2 10 3	17 1½

£ s. d.	£ s. d.	£ s. d.	£ s. d.
3)4 12 6	5)28 2 1	7)24 4 4	8)96 18 9½

		£	s.	d.				£	s.	d.
9.	Divide	56	10	7½	by	5	Quotient	11	6	1½
10.	——	27	18	6	by	8	——	3	9	9¾
11.	——	32	14	0	by	9	——	3	12	8
12.	——	3	15	0	by	10	——		7	6
13.	——	182	16	8	by	12	——	15	4	8½+8
14.	——	170	0	0	by	6	——	28	6	8
15.	——		89		by	8	——		11	1½
16.	——			97	by	2	——			48½

WEIGHTS AND MEASURES.

lb.	*oz.*	*dwt.*	*gr.*
2)25	9	15	20

T.	*cwt.*	*qr.*	*lb.*	*oz.*	*dr.*
3)45	18	3	25	12	3

L.	*M.*	*fur.*	*P.*
4)360	2	4	12

yds.	*ft.*	*in.*
5(960	2	9

yds. qr. na.	yds. qrs. na.	A. R. P.
6)75 0 0	7)994 3 2	8)84 3 16

yds. ft. in.	T. hhd. gal. qt. pt.	bu. pe. qt.
6)72 6 142	9)126 3 40 2 1	10)987 3 2

Y. mo.	W. D. H. min. sec.
11)848 10	12)24 6 20 32 25

When the divisor is the exact product of some two factors in the multiplication table, work by

RULE 2.

Divide by one of said factors, and then divide the quotient by the other factor. If remainders from the lowest denomination occur, proceed with them as directed in note 2, in Simple Division.

EXAMPLES.

1. Divide 72*L.* 16*s.* 7½*d.* by 24. Quotient 3*L.* 0*s.* 8¼*d.* ×6

	L.	*s.*	*d.*			*L.*	*s.*	*d.*	
	4)72	16	7½			6)72	16	7½	
	6)18	4	1¾+2	6 R.		4)12	2	9¼	6
Quotient	3	0	8¼+1		Proof	3	0	8¼+1	

	L.	*s.*	*d.*			*L.*	*s.*	*d.*
2. Divide	29	15	0	by 21	Quotient	1	8	4
3. ——	30	10	10½	by 27	——	1	2	7½
4. ——	134	18	8	by 44	——	3	1	4
5. ——	53	10	0	by 84	——		12	8¾+36
6. ——	984	0	0	by 144	——	6	16	8

When the divisor is more than 12, and not the exact product of any two factors in the multiplication table, work by

RULE 3.

Divide tne highest denomination of the given sum, by rule 2 of Simple Division, and reduce the remainder, if any, to the next lower denomination, adding to it, when reduced, the number there is of that denomination in the given sum; then divide as before, and so proceed.

EXAMPLES.

Divide 36*L.* 16*s.* 3*d.* by 19. Quotient 1*L.* 18*s.* 9*d.*

```
    L.  s.  d.  L.  s.  d.
19)36  16   3 (1   18   9
   19
  ----                          L.  s.  d.
   17                            1  18  9×1
    20                                  6
  ----                         ----------
19)356(18s.                     11  12  6
   19                                   3
  ----                         ----------
   166                          34  17  6
   152                           1  18  9
  ----                         ----------
    14                    Proof 36  16  3
    12                         ----------
  ----
19)171(9d.
   171
  ----
```

	L.	s.	d.				L.	s.	d.
2. Divide	113	13	4	by	31	Quotient	3	13	4
3. ——	189	14	0	by	95	——	1	19	11+
4. ——	38	17	5½	by	47	——		16	6½
5. ——	132	0	8	by	68	——	1	18	10
6. ——	3236	12	4½	by	654	——	4	18	11¾
7. ——		250		by	48	——		5	2½
8. ——			3528	by	32	——			110¼

APPLICATION.

1. Sold 3 yards of muslin for 3 L. 9 s. 6 d., what was the price per yard? Ans. 1 L. 3 s. 2 d.

2. paid 17 s. 6 d. for 4 bushels of salt: how much was it per bushel? Ans. 4 s. 4½ d.

3. If 8 pounds of sugar be sold for 10 s. 6 d., what is the price per pound? Ans. 1 s. 3¾ d.

4. Bought 8 yards of linen for 3L. 11s. 8d. What was the price per yard Ans. 8s. 11½d.

5. Sold 132 yards of cloth for 221L. 18s. 6d. How much was it per yard? Ans. 1L. 13s. 7½d.

6. What is the price of a bushel of wheat, when 42 bushels are sold for 17L. 13s. 6d.? Ans. 8s. 5d.

PROMISCUOUS QUESTIONS.

1. Bought 2 pieces of linen, one of which contained 30 yards, and the other 25 yards; the price was 7s. 6d. per yard: what was the cost of the two pieces?

Ans. 20L. 12s. 6d.

2. Sold one piece of cloth, containing 41 yards, at 2L. 18s. per yard; and another piece containing 36 yards, at 2L. 6s. 6d. per yard: what is the amount of the whole? Ans. 202L. 12s.

3. A person has 500L. 18s. 9d. He owes to one man 25L. 10s.; to another, 76L. 18s. 9d.; to another, 175L. 10s.; and to another, 100L. What sum will he have left after paying these debts? Ans. 123L.

4. A grocer has 10 bags of coffee, weighing each 120 pounds, and 2 bags, weighing each 160 pounds. If he sells 560 pounds, what quantity will remain?

Ans. 960lb.

5. Bought 4 pieces of linen, containing 25 yards, 3 quarters, each, and 3 pieces containing 32 yards, 2 quarters, each; from which was afterwards sold 125 yards: what number of yards was then remaining?

Ans. 75yds. 2qrs.

6. A farmer has three tracts of land, the first contains 125 acres, 3 roods; the second, 200 acres, 2 roods, 18 perches; the third, 175 acres, 10 perches. He intends dividing this land equally between his two sons: what will be the share of each son? Ans. 250A. 2R. 34P.

7. A person, at his decease, left property to the amount of 2425L. 19s. His will directed that 200 pounds should be given to the poor, and that the remainder should be divided, equally, amongst his 3 daughters. What is the portion of each daughter?

Ans. 741£ 19s. 8d.

8. Bought 10 yards of muslin, at 3 s. per yard; 6 yards of tape, at 3 d. per yard: and 7 yards of linen, at 7 s. 6 d. per yard: how much did the whole amount to?

Ans. 4 L. 4 s.

9. Sold 19 bushels of wheat, at $2 37½ per bushel; 15 bushels of rye, at 75 cents per bushel; and 95 bushels of Indian corn, at 87½ cents per bushel: how much did the whole sale amount to? Ans. $139.50.

10. If I buy 15 pounds of sugar, at 10½ cents per lb., and 17 pounds of rice, at 5½ cents per pound, and 19 pounds of candles, at 17¼ cents per pound; how much must I pay for the whole? Ans. $5.78¾.

11. What is the amount of the following bill?

Philadelphia.

James Johnson,

Bought of Samuel Williams,

7 yards of coating	at 17 s.	6 d.	a yard.
18 —— of broad cloth	at 45		——
9 —— ditto	at 48	9	——
23 —— of cassimere	at 18	4½	——
37 —— ditto	at 21	6	——
107 ——drugget	at 9	6	——

Ans. £180 5 10½

A TABLE.

Of Foreign Coins, &c., with their value in Federal money, as established by a late Act of Congress.

	D.	*c.*	*m.*
Pound Sterling, - - - - - -	4,	44	4
Pound of Ireland, - - - - -	4,	10	0
Pagoda of India, - - - -	1,	94	0
Tale of China, - - - - - -	1,	48	0
Mill-ree of Portugal, - - - -	1,	24	0
Ruble of Russia, - - - -	0,	66	0
Rupee of Bengal, - - - - -	0,	55	5
The Guilder of the United Netherlands,	0,	39	0
Mark Banco of Hamburgh, - - -	0,	33	5
Livre Tournois of France, - - - -	0,	18	5
Real Plate of Spain, - - - - -	0,	10	0

A TABLE OF COINS

Which pass current in the United States of North America, with their Sterling and Federal Value

NAMES OF COINS.	Standard weight.		Sterling Money of Great Britain.			New-Hampshire, Massachusetts, Rhode Island, Connecticut, and Virginia.			New-York and North Carolina.			New-Jersey, Pennsylvania, Delaware, and Maryland.			South Carolina and Georgia.			Federal value		
																		Dollars	Cents	Mills
GOLD.	*dwt.*	*gr.*	*L.*	*s.*	*d.*	*L.*	*s.*	*d.*	*L.*	*s.*	*d.*	*L.*	*s.*	*d.*	*L.*	*s.*	*d.*	*D.*	*C.*	*M.*
A Johannes, - - - - -	18		3	12	0	4	16	0	6	8	0	6	0	0	4	0	0	16	00	0
An half Johannes, - -	9	0	1	16	0	2	8	0	3	4	0	3	0	0	2	0	0	8	00	0
A Doubloon, - - - - -	16	21	3	6	0	4	8	0	5	16	0	5	12	6	3	10	0	14	93	3
A Moidore, - - - - - -	6	18	1	7	0	1	16	0	2	8	0	2	5	0	1	8	0	6	00	0
An English Guinea, - -	5	6	1	1	0	1	8	0	1	17	0	1	15	0	1	1	9	4	66	7
A French Guinea, - -	5	5	1	1	0	1	7	6	1	16	0	1	14	6	1	1	5	4	60	0
A Spanish Pistole, - -	4	6	0	16	6	1	2	0	1	9	0	1	8	0	0	18	0	3	77	3
A French Pistole, - -	4	4	0	16	0	1	2	0	1	8	0	1	7	6	0	17	6	3	66	7
SILVER.																				
An English or French Crown, - - - - - -	18	0	0	5	0	0	6	8	0	8	9	0	8	3	0	5	0	1	10	0
The Dollar of Spain, Sweden, or Denmark, - -	17	6	0	4	6	0	6	0	0	8	0	0	7	6	0	4	8	1	00	0
An English Shilling, - -	3	18	0	1	0	0	1	4	0	1	9	0	1	8	0	1	1	0	22	2
A Pistareen, - - - -	3	11	0	0	10¾	0	1	2	0	1	7	0	1	6	0	0	11	0	20	0

*** All other Gold Coins of equal fineness, at 89 cents *per dwt.*, and Silver at 111 cents *per oz.*

COMPOUND REDUCTION.

Compound Reduction teaches to change any sum or quantity which consists of several denominations, to a given denomination; and to change a sum of one kind of money to a given denomination of another kind.

When a sum or quantity, consisting of several denominations, is to be changed to a given denomination, work by the following

RULE.

Reduce the highest denomination to the next lower one, and this again to the next lower, and so on; observing to add to the amount of each denomination the number there is of that denomination in the given sum or quantity.

EXAMPLES.

MONEY.

Reduce $25L.\ 10s.\ 6\frac{3}{4}d.$ to farthings.

L.	*s.*	*d.*
25	10	$6\frac{3}{4}$
20		
500		
10		
510		
12		
6120		
6		
6126		
4		
24504		
3		
24507 farthings.		

Or thus,*

L.	*s.*	*d.*
25	10	$6\frac{3}{4}$
20		
510		
12		
6126		
4		
24507		

qrs.
4)24507
12)6126+3
2|0)51|0+6
Proof $25L.\ 10s.\ 6\frac{3}{4}d.$

---

* The former of these two operations is given merely to render the application of the rule more intelligible: the method of adding in the denominations of the sum, as in the latter operation, should be explained to the scholar.

2. Reduce 36 L. 15 s. to shillings. Facit 735 s.
3. Reduce 32 L. 12 s. 4 d. to pence. Result 7828 d.
4. Bring 102 L. 19 s. $7\frac{1}{4}$ d. to farthings. Result 98861 qrs.
5. Bring 21 L. 10 s. $6\frac{1}{2}$ d. to farthings. Result 20666 qrs.
6. Reduce 137 L. 15 s. $6\frac{3}{4}$ d. to farthings. Result 132267 qrs.
7. Bring 45 L. 3 s. $1\frac{1}{2}$ d. to halfpence. Result 21675 halfpence.
8. Bring 10 L. 10 s. to halfpence Result 5040 halfp.
9. Bring 5 L. 6 s. to farthings. Result 5088 qrs.
10. Bring 2 L. 0 s. $6\frac{1}{4}$ d. to farthings. Facit 1945 qrs.
11. Bring 6 s. $6\frac{1}{4}$ d. to farthings. Facit 313 qrs.

Note 1.—A sum of Federal Money, which consists of dollars and cents, is reduced to cents, by simply removing the separating point.

12. Reduce $25.50 to cents. Facit 2550 cts.
13. Bring $456.05 to cents. Result 45605 cts.
14. Bring $967.10 to cents. Result 96710 cts.

Note 2.—To reduce a sum which consists of dollars and cents, to fourths, thirds, or halves of a cent, &c., reduce it first to cents as in the foregoing examples, then reduce those cents to fourths, thirds, or halves, &c., as under rule 1, note 2, Simple Reduction.

15. Reduce $5.25 to fourths or quarters of a cent. Facit 2100 fourths.
16. Bring 10.18\frac{3}{4}$ to fourths of a cent. Result 4075 fourths.
17. Bring 95.12\frac{1}{2}$ to fourths of a cent. Result 38050 fourths.
18. Reduce 17.33\frac{1}{3}$ to thirds of a cent. Result 5200 thirds.
19. Reduce 56.66\frac{2}{3}$ to thirds of a cent. Result 17000 thirds.
20. Bring $420.10 to half cents. Facit 84020 halves.
21. Bring 375.12\frac{1}{2}$ to half cents. Result 75025 halves.

Note 3.—To reduce pence, Pennsylvania currency,* to cents, annex a cypher to their number, and divide by 9. To reduce pence to mills, annex two cyphers, and divide by 9.

---

* The same rule that applies to Pennsylvania currency applies also to the currencies of New Jersey, Delaware, and Maryland.

22. Reduce 1575 pence to cents. Facit 1750 cts.

```
9)15750
  ─────
   1750 cents.
```

23. Bring 4725 pence to cents. Result 5250 cts.
24. Bring 3150 pence to cents. Result 3500 cts.
25. Reduce 1575 pence to mills. Facit 17500 mills.

Note 4.—To change pounds, Pennsylvania currency, to Federal Money, annex two cyphers to their number, then multiply by 8, and divide the product by 3; the quotient will be cents, which reduce to dollars.

26. Reduce 25 pounds to dollars Facit $\$66.66\frac{2}{3}$

```
   2500
      8
  ─────
3)20000
  ─────
 $66.66⅔
```

27. Bring 150 pounds to dollars. Result $400.00.
28. Bring 756 pounds to dollars. Result $2016.00.
29. Bring 17 pounds to dollars. Result $\$45.33\frac{1}{3}$.

If there are shillings, or shillings and pence, with the pounds, reduce the whole to pence; then reduce those pence to cents, and the cents to dollars.

30. Reduce 156 pounds, 6 shillings, to dollars. Facit $416.80.

31. Bring 29 pounds, 12 shillings, to dollars. Result $\$78.93\frac{1}{3}$.

32. Bring 100 pounds, 12 shillings, and 6 pence, to dollars. Result $\$268.33\frac{1}{3}$.

Note 5.—To reduce cents to pence, Pennsylvania currency, multiply by 9, and separate one figure from the right of the product.

33. Reduce 359 cents to pence. Result 323 pence.

```
 359
   9
─────
323|1
```

34. Bring 89 cents to pence. Facit 80 pence.
35. Bring 350 cents to pence. Facit 315 pence.

Note 6.—To reduce dollars, or dollars and cents, to pounds, Pennsylvania currency, reduce them first to cents, then reduce those cents to pence, and then reduce those pence to pounds.

36. Reduce $68.30 to pounds.

```
      6830
         9
    ------
 12)6147|0
    ------
2|0)51|2 3
```

Result 25 L. 12 s. 3 d.

37. Bring $450 to pounds.

```
      45000
          9
    -------
 12)40500|0
    -------
 2|0)337|5
```

Result 168 L. 15 s.

38. Reduce 125 dollars to pounds. Facit 46L. 17s. 6d.
39. Bring $246.29 to pounds. Result 92 L. 7 s. 2 d.
40. Bring 728 dollars to pounds. Result 273 L.
41. Bring $79.60 to pounds. Result 29 L. 17 s.

Note 7.—To reduce pounds sterling to Federal Money, bring them to sixpences, or to pence, and to these annex two cyphers; then, if sixpences, divide by 9, but if pence, divide by 54, and the quotient will be cents, which reduce to dollars.

42. Reduce 230 L. 15 s. 6 d. sterling to Federal Money.

```
   230 L. 15 s. 6 d.
    20
  ----
  4615
     2
  ----
9)923100
  ------
```

Result $1025.66½+

43. Reduce 218 L. 19 s. 6 d. sterling to Federal Money. Facit $973.22+
44. Bring 25 L. sterling to Federal Money. Result $111.11+
45. Bring 437 L. 18 s. sterling to Federal Money. Facit 1946 dols. 22 cts.

Note 8.—A general rule to change the currency of each of the States to Federal Money.

Reduce the given sum to shillings, or to sixpences, or to pence, and to these annex two cyphers; then divide by the number of shillings, sixpences, or pence in a dollar, as it passes in each State: the quotient will be cents. (For the value of a dollar, see the table at page 63.)

46. Reduce 63 L. 15 s., New England or Virginia currency, to Federal Money, a dollar being 6 s.
Facit $212.50.

47. Reduce 112 L. 16 s., New York or North Carolina currency, to Federal Money. Result $282.00.

48. Reduce 161 L. 14 s., South Carolina or Georgia currency, to Federal Money. Result $693.00

WEIGHTS AND MEASURES.

1. Reduce 47 pounds, 10 ounces, 15 pennyweights, to pennyweights. Facit 11495 dwt.
2. Reduce 5 lb. 6 oz. 4 dwt. 20 gr. to grains.
Result 31796 gr.
3. Bring 2 tons, 15 cwt. 2 quarters, to quarters.
Result 222 qrs.
4. Bring 3 tons, 25 lb. to pounds. Result 6745 lb.
5. Reduce 7 cwt. 3 qrs. 10 lb. to ounces.
Facit 14048 oz.
6. Bring 27 ℔ 7 ℥ 2 ʒ 1 ℈ 2 grs. to grains.
Result 159022 grs.
7. Bring 3 leagues, 2 miles, 7 furlongs, to furlongs.
Result 95 fur.
8. Bring 57 miles, 2 furlongs, to poles.
Result 18320 P.
9. Reduce 15 yards, 2 feet, to inches. Result 564 in.
10. Bring 42 English ells, 3 quarters, to quarters.
Result 213 qrs.
11. Bring 17 yards, 2 quarters, 2 nails, to nails.
Result 282 na.
12. Reduce 11 acres, 2 roods, 19 perches, to perches.
Result 1859 P.
13. Bring 17 acres, 3 roods, to perches. Result 2840 P.

14. Reduce 14 tuns, 3 hogsheads, to hogsheads. Result 59 hhd.

15. Reduce 2 hogsheads, 10 gallons, to quarts. Result 544 qt.

16. Bring 40 gallons, 3 quarts, 1 pint, to pints. Result 327 pt.

17. Bring 16 bushels, 1 peck, to pecks. Result 65 pe.

18. Bring 15 bushels, 6 quarts, to quarts. Facit 486 qt.

19. Reduce 18 years, 6 months, to months. Result 222 mo.

20. Bring 3 weeks, 4 days, to days. Result 25 D.

21. Bring 2 weeks, 20 hours, to minutes. Result 21360 min.

PROMISCUOUS QUESTIONS.

1. How many shillings are there in 45 pounds, 10 shillings? Ans. 910 s.

2. How many cents are there in 630 pence, Pennsylvania currency? Ans. 700 cts.

3. What number of farthings do 18 s. 6 d. make? Ans. 888 far.

4. How many pence is there in 4 L. 5 s. 4 d.? Ans. 1024 d.

5. How many dollars are there in 37 L. 10 s., Pennsylvania currency? Ans. $100.

6. In 1400 cents, how many pence, Pennsylvania currency? Ans. 1260 pence.

7. In 64130 cents, how many pounds, Pennsylvania currency? Ans. 240 L. 9 s. 9 d.

8. How many pounds, Pennsylvania currency, are there in 560 dollars? Ans. 210 L.

9. How many dollars are there in 600 pounds, New York currency? Ans. $1500

10. In 38 L. 9 s. 3 d. sterling, how many dollars? Ans. $170.94¼+

11. In 845 French crowns, how many pounds, Pennsylvania currency? Ans. 348 L. 11 s. 3 d.

12. How many spoons weighing each 5 oz. 10 dwt. will 10 lb. 1 oz. of silver make? Ans. 22.

13. A grocer has 34 cwt. 2 qrs. 12 lb. of sugar, and

intends to divide it into parcels, each of which to weigh 68 pounds: how many of these parcels will there be? Ans. 57.

14. In 28 cwt. 3 qrs. 24 lb. how many pounds? Ans. 3244 lb.

15. In 560 poles, how many miles? Ans. 1 M. 6 fur.

16. In 327 English ells of cloth, how many yards? Ans. 408 yds. 3 qrs.

17. How many quarters of a yard are there in 18 yards, 2 quarters? Ans. 74 qrs.

18. A tract of land containing 1299600 square perches, is to be divided into 25 plantations of equal size: how many acres will there be in each? Ans. 324 A. 3 R. 24 P.

19. How many casks which will contain 33 gallons each, may be filled out of 5 pipes and 1 hogshead of cider? Ans. 21.

20. In 15 bushels, 6 qts. how many quarts? Ans. 486.

21. In 10 weeks, 2 days, how many days? Ans. 72.

22. In 17 years, 9 months, how many months? Ans. 213.

23. How many seconds are there in a solar year, which consists of 365 days, 5 hours, 48 minutes, and 58 seconds? Ans. 31556938 sec.

24. How many days from the 24th of the fifth month, (May,) 1797, to the 15th of the twelfth month, (December,) 1798, inclusive? Ans. 571 days.

SIMPLE PROPORTION,

OR

THE SINGLE RULE OF THREE.

Four numbers are said to be proportional, when the first contains the second, or some part of the second, as often as the third contains the fourth, or a like part of the fourth.

In questions which are solved by Simple Proportion, three terms of a proportion are given to find the fourth.

RULE.

Write down, for the third term, that number which is of the same name or kind with the answer.

Consider, from the nature of the question, whether the answer should be greater or less than this third term. If it is to be *greater*, set the greater of the two remaining numbers on the left hand, for the second term, and the other for the first; but if *less*, set the less of those two numbers for the second, and the other for the first.

When the question is thus stated, if the first and second terms be not of the same denomination, reduce one or both of them till they are; and if the third term consist of several denominations, reduce it to its lowest denomination; then,

Multiply the second and third terms together, and divide the product by the first term: the quotient will be the answer.

Note.—The product of the second and third terms is of the same denomination as the third term; and the learner may be reminded, that the quotient and remainder are of the same denomination as the number divided.

See examples 14, 15, and 16, under rule 1, and 7, 8, under rule 3, Compound Division.

The rule which is given above, as it renders the distinctions of *direct* and *inverse* proportion unnecessary, and has several other advantages, is preferable to the one which was formerly used; and it is likely to be generally adopted: but for the convenience of those teachers who have not yet determined to employ it, the last mentioned rule is subjoined.

RULE FOR STATING.

Set that term of the supposition which is of the same name or kind with the term of demand, in the first place, set the other term of supposition in the second place, and the term of demand in the third place.

When the question is thus stated, consider whether the proportion is direct or inverse.

The proportion is direct, when the third term is greater than the first, and the nature of the question requires that the fourth term, or answer, should be greater than the second; or when the third term is less than the first, and it is required that the fourth term be less than the second.

The proportion is inverse, when the third term is greater than the first, and the fourth is to be less than the second; or when the third term is less than the first, and the fourth is to be greater than the second.

PROOF.

Invert the question, making the answer the third term, as in the following wrought examples.

EXAMPLES.

1. If 2 yards of muslin cost 4 shillings, what will 6 yards cost?

yds.		*yds.*		*s.*
2	:	6	: :	4
		4		
	2)24			
	Ans. 12*s*.			

yds.		*yds.*		*s.*
6	:	2	: :	12
				2
				6)24
				Proof 4*s*.

RULE FOR DIRECT PROPORTION.

If the first and third terms be not of the same denomination, reduce both to the lowest in either; and if the second term consist of several denominations, reduce it to its lowest denomination: then, multiply the second and third terms together, and divide the product by the first term; the quotient will be the fourth term, or answer, in the same denomination as the second, or that to which the second was reduced.

EXAMPLE.

If 2 yards of muslin cost 4 shillings, what will 6 yards cost?

yds.		*s.*		*yds.*
2	:	4	: :	6
				4
				2)24
				12 Answer.

RULE FOR INVERSE PROPORTION.

Multiply the first and second terms together, and divide the product by the third; the quotient will be the answer in the same denomination as the second, or that to which the second was reduced.

EXAMPLE.

If 4 men can build a wall in 4 days, how many men can do it in 8 days.

men.		*days.*		*days.*
4	:	4	: :	8
		4		
		8)16		
		2 Answer.		

2. If 10 shillings will pay for 20 pounds of beef, how many pounds will 5s. pay for?

s.	*s.*	*lb.*	*s.*	*s.*	*lb.*
10 :	5 ::	20	5 :	10 ::	10
		5		10	
		10)100		5)100	
		Ans. 10 *lb.*		Proof 20 *lb.*	

3. If 1lb. of sugar cost 9d., what will 2cwt. 2qrs. 10lb. cost?

lb. *cwt. qrs. lb.* *d.* *cwt. qrs. lb.* *lb.* *L. s. d.*
1 : 2 2 10 :: 9 2 2 10 : 1 :: 10 17 6

4	4	20
10	10	217
28	28	12
80	80	290)2610(9d.Pr.
21	21	2610
290 lb.	290	
9		
12)2610 pence.		
2|0)21|7 6		

Ans. 10 L. 17s. 6d.

4. Sold 125 bushels of wheat, at 11 s. 3 d. a bushel; what did it come to? Ans. 70 L. 6 s. 2 d.

bu. *bu.* *s. d.* *bu.* *bu.* *L. s. d.*
1 : 125 :: 11 3 125 : 1 :: 70 6 3

12	20	
135	1406	
125	12	
675	125)16875(12|135	
270	125	
135		Pr. 11s. 3d.
	437	
12)16875 pence	375	
2|0)140|6 3	625	
	625	
Ans. 70 L. 6 s. 3 d.		

5. If 3 pounds of sugar cost 4 shillings, what will 6 pounds cost? Ans. 8 s.

6. If 8 yards of muslin cost 24 shillings, what will 96 yards come to? Ans. 14 L. 8 s.

7. If 12 bushels of wheat be worth 16 dollars, how much are 48 bushels worth? Ans. 64 dols.

8. If 1 pound of butter bring 16 pence, what will 56 pounds bring? Ans. 3 L. 14 s. 8 d.

9. Sold 12 yards of cloth for 72 dollars: how much was it per yard? Ans. 6 dols.

10. If 12 yards of cloth cost 19 L. 16 s., what will 192 yards come to? Ans. 316 L. 16 s.

11. If 96 pounds of sugar cost 3 L. 12 s., what is it per pound? Ans. 9 d.

12. What will 421 bushels of wheat come to, at 1 dollar 35 cents per bushel? Ans. $568 35.

13. What will 128 pounds of pork come to, at 8 cents a pound? Ans. 10 dols. 24 cts.

14. How much will 75 pounds of almonds come to, at 37½ cents a pound? Ans. $28.12½.

15. If 3 yards of cloth cost 5 L. 12 s. 6 d., how much will 225 yards cost? Ans. 421 L. 17 s. 6 d.

16. If 1 pound of rice cost 4⅓ d., what will 48 pounds cost? Ans. 18 s.

17. Bought 230 bushels of coal for 26 L. 16 s. 8 d., how much was it per bushel? Ans. 2 s. 4 d.

18. Bought 120 bushels of corn for 58 dollars: how much is that a bushel? Ans. 48⅓ cts.

19. If 891 gallons of molasses cost 176 L. 6 s. 10 ½., what is it per gallon? Ans. 3 s. 11½ d.

20. What must be paid for 45 bushels, 3 pecks of potatoes, at 2 s. 8 d. a bushel? Ans. 6 L. 2 s.

21. If 1 dozen of penknives cost two dollars 50 cents, how much will 4 dozen come to? Ans. $10.00.

22. If the price of 1 acre of land be 18 dollars, 25 cents, what will 50 acres, 2 roods, 20 perches come to? Ans. $923.90½+

23. If 1 hundred weight of sugar cost 2 L. 11 s. 4 d., what is the price of 1 pound? Ans. 5½d.

24. If 1 hundred weight of iron be worth 1 L. 8 s., what is the value of 33cwt. 1qr. 22lb.? Ans. 46L. 16s. 6d.

25. Sold 3 hundred weight of tobacco, at 18 d. per

pound, what did it amount to? Ans. 25 L. 4 s.

26. If 19 dozen pair of stockings cost 136 dols. 80 cents, what is the cost of 1 pair? Ans. 60 cts.

27. Bought 6 cwt. of sugar at 10 cents a pound: what does it amount to? Ans. $67.20.

28. A silversmith bought 73 lb. 5 oz. 15 dwt. of silver, for which he paid 5s. 9d. per ounce; what was the amount? Ans. 253 L. 10 s. 0¾ d.

29. A French crown is 8 s. 3 d., Pennsylvania currency: how many pounds of that currency are 100 French crowns? Ans. 41 L. 5 s.

30. What must be paid for 53 English ells, 3 quarters of linen, at the rate of 7 s. 9½ d. per yard?
Ans. 26 L. 2 s. 0½ d.

31. If 1 yard of muslin cost 21 cents, what will 43½ yards cost? Ans. $9.13½.

32. If 1½ yards of silk cost 2 dollars, 50 cents, what will 1 quarter, 2 nails cost? Ans. 62½ cts.

33. What is the value of 5½ pounds of tea, at 9 s. 4½ d. per pound? Ans. 2 L. 11 s. 6¾ d.

34. What is the value of 795 pounds of coffee, at 24½ cents a pound? Ans. $194.77½.

35. Calculate the amount of 1475 bushels of Indian corn, at 87½ cents a bushel? Facit $1290.62½.

36. What must be paid for 53 English ells, 1 quarter of Holland, at the rate of 7 s. 9½ d. per yard?
Ans. 25 L. 18 s. 1¾ d.

37. What will a hogshead of sugar come to, weighing 7 cwt. 3 qrs., at 10 dollars 62½ cents per hundred weight? Ans. $82.34⅓.

38. If 5 yards of cloth cost 28 s. 4 d., what is the value of 18 pieces, each containing 21 yards, 1 quarter?
Ans. 108 L. 7 s. 6 d.

39. What must be paid for 7 casks of prunes, each weighing 4 cwt. 3 qrs., at 2 L. 19 s. 8 d. per hundred?
Ans. 99 L. 3 s. 11 d

40. If I buy 20 pieces of cloth, each 20 ells, for 12s. 6d. per ell, what is the amount of the whole? Ans. 250L.

41. What will four pieces of cloth come to, containing 23, 24, 25, and 27 yards, at 72 cents per yard?
Ans. $71.28.

42. Bought 3 pipes of wine, containing 120½, 124,

$126\frac{3}{4}$ gallons, at 5 s. 6 d. per gallon: what did they amount to? Ans. 102 L. 1 s. $10\frac{1}{2}$ d.

43. Bought 4 pieces of linen, two of which contained $27\frac{1}{2}$ yards each, and the other two $25\frac{3}{4}$ yards each, at $62\frac{1}{2}$ cents per yard: what was the cost? Ans. \$66.56$\frac{1}{4}$.

44. If the price of 1 yard of muslin be 3s., what number of yards may be bought with 1L.17s.6d.? Ans. $12\frac{1}{2}$yds.

45. What quantity of sugar will 23 L. 10 s. buy, at 26 s. 8 d. per hundred weight? Ans. 17 cwt. 2 qrs. 14lb.

46. A person bought a piece of cloth for 16 L. 10 s., the price of which, per yard, was 15 s.: how many yards did it contain? Ans. 22 yards.

47. If a person have a salary of 1333 dollars a year, and spend daily 2 dollars, 14 cents, how much will he save each year? Ans. \$551.90

48. If a person's income be 890 dollars, 50 cents, a year, how much may he spend each day, to save every year 120 dols. 35 cts. Ans. \$2.11.

49. If a staff 4 feet long cast a shade (on level ground) 7 feet long, what is the height of a steeple whose shade at the same time is 198 feet? Ans. $113\frac{1}{7}$ feet.

Note.—The operation may frequently be contracted, by dividing the dividing term, and either of the other two, one by the other, or by any number that will divide them both without a remainder, using their quotients in their stead, as in the following examples.

50. If 24 yards of muslin cost 60 shillings, how much will 4 yards cost?

yds.	*yds.*	*s.*	(12) *yds.*	*yds.*	*s.*	(12) *yds.*	*yds.*	*s.*
24 :	4 : :	60	24 :	4 : :	60	24 :	4 : :	60
6		10s. Ans.	2		5	2	2	5
					4			2
Thus, 24 ÷ 4 = 6					—			—
And 60 ÷ 6 = 10					2)20			Ans. 10s.
					—			
					10s. Ans.			

51. If 36 yards of linen cost 90s., what will 12 yards cost? Ans. 30s.

52. If 24 yards of check cost 60s., what will 8 yards cost? Ans. 20s.

53. What will 12 gallons of oil come to, if 6 gallons cost 18s.? Ans. 36s.

54. If 8 yards of velvet cost $3.20, what will 96 yards come to? Ans. $38.40.

55. If 9 lb. of sugar cost 9 s. 4 d., what is the value of 27 lb.? Ans. 1 L. 8 s.

56. How much will 60 bushels of apples come to, if 4 bushels cost 1 L. 4 s.? Ans. 18 L.

INVERSE PROPORTION.

Questions in Inverse Proportion may be solved precisely in the same manner as the foregoing examples.

EXAMPLES.

1. If 12 men can build a house in 48 days, in what time could 36 men build it? Ans. 16 days.

2. If 48 men can build a wall in 24 days, how many men can do it in 192 days? Ans. 6 men.

3. If 100 men can finish a piece of work in 12 days, how many can do it in 3 days? Ans. 400 men.

4. How many laborers must be employed to finish a piece of work in 15 days, which 5 can do in 24 days? Ans. 8.

5. If 6 reapers can reap a field of wheat in 12 days, in what time could 24 do it? Ans. 3 days.

6. If 100 dollars in 12 months bring 6 dollars interest, what sum will bring the same in 8 months? Ans. $150.

7. If a footman perform a journey in 3 days, when the days are 16 hours long, how many days will he require of 12 hours long, to perform the same in? Ans. 4.

8. How many yards of matting, 2 feet 6 inches broad, will cover a floor that is 27 feet long, and 20 feet broad? Ans. 72 yards.

9. What quantity of shalloon, that is 3 quarters of a yard wide, will line $7\frac{1}{2}$ yards of cloth, that is $1\frac{1}{2}$ yards wide? Ans. 15 yards.

10. How many yards of carpeting, that is 3 quarters of a yard wide, are sufficient to cover a floor that is 18 feet wide, and 60 feet long? Ans. 160 yds.

11. If a board be 9 inches broad, how long must it be to measure 12 square feet? Ans. 16 feet.

12. How much in length that is $4\frac{1}{2}$ inches broad will make a square foot? Ans. 32 inches.

PROMISCUOUS EXAMPLES.

1. Calculate the value of $26\frac{1}{2}$ yards of linen, at 5 s. 6 d. a yard? Facit 7 L. 5 s. 9 d.

2. Purchased 156 lb. of soap for 15 dollars 60 cents: what was the price per pound? Ans. 10 cts.

3. How many yards of cloth, 3 quarters of a yard wide, are equal in measure to 30 yards, of 5 quarters wide? Ans. 50 yards.

4. Bought $27\frac{1}{4}$ yards of muslin, at 6 s. $9\frac{1}{2}$ d. per yard: what does it amount to? Ans. 9 L. 5 s. $0\frac{3}{4}$ d. + 2.

5. In what time will 600 dollars gain the interest which 80 dollars would gain in 15 years? Ans. 2 years.

6. What quantity of wine, at 6 s. per gallon, may be bought with 18 L. 18 s.? Ans. 63 gals.

7. If 1 hundred weight of sugar cost 13 dollars 50 cents, what must be paid for 17 cwt. 3 qrs. 14 lb.? Ans. $241.31\frac{1}{4}$ cents.

8. A cistern has a pipe which will empty it in 10 hours: how many pipes of the same capacity will empty it in 30 minutes? Ans. 20.

9. How many yards of paper, $2\frac{1}{2}$ feet wide, will be required to cover a wall which is 12 feet long, and 9 feet high? Ans. 14 yds. 1 ft. 2 in.

10. If $1\frac{1}{2}$ oz. of spice cost $6\frac{1}{4}$ d., what will $3\frac{1}{4}$ oz. cost at the same rate? Ans. 1 s. $1\frac{1}{2}$ d. +

11. What is the value of a piece of cloth containing 52 English ells, 3 quarters, at 1 dollar 76 cents per yard? Ans. $115.72.

COMPOUND PROPORTION,

OR

THE DOUBLE RULE OF THREE.

Compound Proportion is compounded of two or more ranks of proportionals; five, seven, nine, &c., terms being given, to find a sixth, eighth, &c.

RULE.

Work by two or more statings in Simple Proportion; or,

Set that term which is like the term sought, in the

third place, and consider each pair of similar terms and this third one, as the terms of a stating in Simple Proportion, and set them severally, in the first and second places, agreeably to the directions under that rule.

When the question is thus stated, reduce the similar terms to like denominations, and then multiply all the terms in the second and third places together, and divide the product by the product of those in the first place, the quotient will be the answer, or term sought.

The above rule is preferred for reasons similar to those which have been given for adopting the new rule for Simple Proportion: the one formerly used is, however, subjoined.

RULE FOR STATING.

Set the two terms of supposition which are of the same name or kind as those of the demand, one under the other, in the first place; that of the same kind as the answer in the second, and those of the demand in the third, with the two corresponding terms of the supposition and demand opposite to each other, and of the same denomination.

When a question is stated, consider the two upper terms with the middle one, as a stating in the Single Rule of Three, and also the two under terms, with the middle one, as a stating in the same rule; if, in both instances, the proportion be direct, the question is in direct proportion; but if in either of them the proportion be inverse, the question is in inverse proportion.

RULE FOR DIRECT PROPORTION.

Multiply the two terms in the third place together, and multiply the product by the middle term; divide the last product by the product of the terms in the first place, and the quotient will be the answer, in the same denomination as the middle term.

EXAMPLE.

If 6 men in 8 days eat 10 lb. of bread, how much will 12 men eat in 24 days? Ans. 60.

```
6 men  }          { 12 men                Contracted.
8 days } 10 lb.   { 24 days        6̸ }         { 1̸2̸  2
                    --             8̸ }  10     { 2̸4̸  3
                    48                               --
                   24                                 6
                   ---                               10
                   288                               --
                    10                            60 lb.
                   ----
              48)2880(60 lb.
                 288
                 ---
                   0
```

PROOF.

By two statings in the Single Rule of Three.

Note.—if either of the two first terms, or both, will divide, or can be divided by any of the three last, or if any other number will divide one of the first and one of the last, without a remainder, the operation may be contracted by using their quotients in their stead.

EXAMPLES.

1. If 6 men in 8 days eat 10 lb. of bread, how much will 12 men eat in 24 days? Ans. 60.

```
men  6 : 12 }
days 8 : 24 } :: 10 lb.
        ---
        288
         10
        ---
    48)2880(60 Ans.
        288
        ---
          0
```

Contracted.

```
6 : 12 2 }
8 : 24 3 } :: 10 lb.
        ---
          6
         10
         --
         60 Ans.
```

2. If 3 men in 4 days eat 5 lb. of bread, how much will suffice 6 men for 12 days? Ans. 30 lb.

3. Suppose 4 men in 12 days mow 48 acres, how many acres can 8 men mow in 16 days? Ans. 128 A.

RULE FOR INVERSE PROPORTION.

Transpose the inverse extremes; that is, set that which is in the first place under the third; and that which is in the third place under the first; then work as in Direct Proportion.

EXAMPLE.

If 7 men reap 84 acres of wheat in 12 days, how many men can reap 100 acres in 5 days? Ans. 20.

```
84 A. }       { 100 direct
12 D. } 7 m.  {   5 inverse
 5    }       {  12
---             ----
420             1200
                   7
                ----
           420)8400(20
               840
               ---
                 0
```

Contracted.

```
)84 }       { 100(20 Ans
 12 }  7m.  {   5
  5 }       {  12
  7 }       {
```

4. If 10 bushels of oats be sufficient for 18 horses 20 days, how many bushels will serve 60 horses 36 days, at that rate? Ans. 60 bu.

5. If 7 quarters of malt are sufficient for a family of 7 persons 4 months, how many quarters will 46 persons use in 10 months? Ans. 115.

6. Suppose the wages of 6 persons for 21 weeks be 288 dollars, what must 14 persons receive for 46 weeks? Ans. 1472 dols.

7. If 8 reapers have 3 L. 4 s. for 4 days work, how much will 48 men have for 16 days work? Ans. 76L. 16s.

8. If 100 L. in 12 months gain 6 L. interest, how much will 75 L. gain in 9 months? Ans. 3 L. 7 s. 6 d.

9. If 100 L. in 52 weeks gain 6 L. interest, how much will 200 L. gain in 26 weeks? Ans. 6 L.

10. If the carriage of 8 cwt. 128 miles cost $12.80, what must be paid for the carriage of 4 cwt. 32 miles? Ans. $1.60.

11. If 16 L. 18 s. be the wages of 16 men for 8 days, what sum will 32 men earn in 24 days? Ans. 101 L. 8 s.

12. If 350 L. in half a year gain 10 L. 10 s. interest, what will be the interest of 400 L. for 4 years? Ans. 96 L.

INVERSE PROPORTION.

1. If 7 men reap 84 acres of wheat in 12 days, how many men can reap 100 acres in 5 days? Ans. 20 men.

2. If 4 dollars be the hire of 8 men for 3 days, how many days must 20 men work for 40 dollars? Ans. 12.

3. If 4 men have $3.20 for 3 days work, how many men will earn $12.80 in 16 days? Ans. 3 men.

4. If 4 reapers have 12 dollars for 3 days work, how many will earn 48 dollars in 16 days? Ans. 3.

5. If 100 L. in 12 months gain 6 L. interest, what sum will gain 3 L. 7 s. 6 d. in 9 months? Ans. 75 L.

6. If a footman travel 240 miles in 12 days, when the days are 12 hours long; how many days will he require to travel 720 miles, when the days are 16 hours long Ans. 27 days.

7. If 100 L. in 12 months gain 8 L. interest, what sum will gain 8 L. 12 s. in 5 months. Ans. 258 L.

8. If 200 lb. be carried 40 miles for 40 cents, how far may 20200 lb. be carried for $60.60? Ans. 60 miles.

PROMISCUOUS EXAMPLES.

1. If 4 men in 5 days eat 7 lb. of bread, how much will suffice 16 men 15 days? Ans. 84 lb.

2. If 100 dols. gain \$3.50 interest in one year, what sum will gain \$38.50 in 1 year and three months? Ans. 880 dols.

3. If it take 5 men to make 150 pair of shoes in 20 days, how many men can make 1350 pair in 60 days? Ans. 15.

4. If the wages of 6 men for 21 weeks be 120 L., what will be the wages of 14 men for 46 weeks? Ans. 613 L. 6 s. 8 d.

5. If 333 L. 6 s. 8 d. gain 15 L. interest in 9 months, what sum will gain 6 L. in 12 months? Ans. 100 L.

6. A wall which is to be built to the height of 27 feet, has been raised 9 feet in 6 days, by 12 men: how many men must be employed to finish the work in 4 days? Ans. 36 men.

PRACTICE.

Practice is a short method of ascertaining the value of any number of articles, or of pounds yards, &c., by the given price of one article, one pound, or one yard, &c.

Practice may be proved by Compound Multiplication, or by the Single Rule of Three Direct.

TABLES OF ALIQUOT PARTS.*

qr.		
1	= $\frac{1}{4}$	of 1*d.*
2	$\frac{1}{2}$	
d.		
1	= $\frac{1}{12}$	of a shilling.
$1\frac{1}{2}$	$\frac{1}{8}$	
2	$\frac{1}{6}$	
3	$\frac{1}{4}$	
4	$\frac{1}{3}$	
6	$\frac{1}{2}$	

s.	*d.*		
1	0	= $\frac{1}{20}$	of a pound.
1	8	$\frac{1}{12}$	
2	0	$\frac{1}{10}$	
2	6	$\frac{1}{8}$	
3	4	$\frac{1}{6}$	
4	0	$\frac{1}{5}$	
5	0	$\frac{1}{4}$	
6	8	$\frac{1}{3}$	
10	0	$\frac{1}{2}$	

cts.		
50	= $\frac{1}{2}$	of a dollar.
25	$\frac{1}{4}$	
20	$\frac{1}{5}$	
$12\frac{1}{2}$	$\frac{1}{8}$	
10	$\frac{1}{10}$	
$6\frac{1}{4}$	$\frac{1}{16}$	

lb.		
7	= $\frac{1}{16}$	of an cwt.
8	$\frac{1}{14}$	
14	$\frac{1}{8}$	
16	$\frac{1}{7}$	
28	$\frac{1}{4}$	
56	$\frac{1}{2}$	

* An aliquot part of a number is any number that will divide it without a remainder; thus 4 is an aliquot part of 20, and 8 of 56. A sum or quantity is an aliquot part of a greater sum or quantity, when a certain number thereof will make the greater: thus a shilling is an aliquot part of a pound, because 20 shillings make one pound.

When the price is less than a penny, work by

RULE 1.

If the price be a farthing, or a halfpenny, set down the value of the given number at a penny, and take such part of that sum as the price is of a penny, for the answer in pence.*

If the price be three farthings, find the value of the given number at a halfpenny, and afterwards at a farthing; then add the two results together, and their amount will be the answer.

*** If the learner be unable to tell the denomination of a quotient, or how to proceed with remainders, it would be useful to refer him to examples 14, 15, and 16, under Rule 1, and 7, 8, under Rule 3, Compound Division.

EXAMPLES.

1. What is the value of 4528 quills, at $\frac{1}{4}$ each?
2. What is the value of 4528 quills, at $\frac{3}{4}$ each?

(1) *d.*

| $\frac{1}{4}$ | $\frac{1}{4}$ | 4528 value at 1 d.

12)1132 Ans. in pence.

2|0)9|4 4

Ans. redu. 4 L. 14 s. 4 d.

(2) *d.*

| $\frac{1}{2}$ | $\frac{1}{2}$ | 4528 value at 1d.
| $\frac{1}{4}$ | $\frac{1}{4}$ |

2264 value at $\frac{1}{2}$
1132 value at $\frac{1}{4}$

12)3396 Ans.

2|0)28|3

Ans. reduced 14 L. 3 s.

			L.	*s.*	*d.*
3.	64 at $\frac{1}{4}$	Answer		1	4
4.	7612 at $\frac{1}{4}$	———	7	18	7
5.	2345 at $\frac{1}{2}$	———	4	17	$8\frac{1}{2}$

* The value of any number of articles at a penny, each, is that number of pence: thus, the value of two things at a penny, each, is two pence: of three things, three pence; of twenty things, twenty pence, &c.; and, as a farthing is the fourth part of a penny, the value at a farthing must be a fourth part of the value at a penny; and as two farthings are the half of a penny, the value at two farthings must be half of the value at a penny, &c.

This explanation of the rule, with a little variation, will apply to most of the other rules of Practice.

			L.	s.	d.
6.	6812 at $\frac{1}{2}$	Answer	14	3	10
7.	1487 at $\frac{3}{4}$	———	4	12	$11\frac{1}{4}$
8.	4712 at $\frac{3}{4}$	———	14	14	6

When the price is not less than a penny, but less than a shilling, and is an aliquot part of a shilling, work by

RULE 2.

Set down the value of the given number at a shilling, and take such part of it as the price is of a shilling, for the answer.

EXAMPLES.

1. What is the value of 7612 lb. of rosin, at 1 d. per lb. and also at $1\frac{1}{2}$ d. per lb.?

| 1 d. | $\frac{1}{12}$ | 7612 s. value at 1 s. | $1\frac{1}{2}$ d. | $\frac{1}{8}$ | 7612 s. value at 1 s.

2|0)63|4 4   2|0)95|1 6

Ans. redu. 31 L. 14 s. 4 d. Ans. reduced 47L. 11 s. 6 d.

	d.		L.	s.	d.
2.	24 at 1	Answer		2	0
3.	3806 at $1\frac{1}{2}$	———	23	15	9
4.	1769 at 2	———	14	14	10
5.	7649 at 3	———	95	12	3
6.	8120 at 4	———	135	6	8
7.	2764 at 6	———	69	2	0

When the price is not less than a penny, but less than a shilling, and is no aliquot part of a shilling, work by

RULE 3.

Separate the price into parts, one of which shall be an aliquot part of a shilling, and the rest either aliquot parts of a shilling or of one of the other parts. Find the value at each of the parts agreeably to the tenor of the preceding rules, and add the several results together, for the answer.

EXAMPLES.

1. What is the value of 6192 yards of tape. at $2\frac{1}{4}$ d. per yard?

2. What is the value of 3711 lb. of sugar, at $7\frac{3}{4}$ d. per lb.?

(1.)			s.	
	2d.	$\frac{1}{6}$	6192	value at 1 s.
	$\frac{1}{4}$	$\frac{1}{8}$	1032	value at 2 d.
			129	value at $\frac{1}{4}$.
			2|0)116|1	Answer in shillings.

Answer reduced 58 L. 1 s.

(2.)					
	4d.	$\frac{1}{3}$	3711		value at 1 s.
	3d.	$\frac{1}{4}$			
			1237		at 4 d.
	$\frac{1}{2}$	$\frac{1}{6}$	927	9	at 3 d.
	$\frac{1}{4}$	$\frac{1}{2}$	154	$7\frac{1}{2}$	at $\frac{1}{2}$.
			77	$3\frac{3}{4}$	at $\frac{1}{4}$.
			2|0)239|6	$8\frac{1}{4}$	Ans. in shillings, &c.

Answer reduced 119 L. 16 s. $8\frac{1}{4}$ d.

Note.—In working the former of these examples, we find the value of the given number at 2 d. by Rule 2, and divide the result by 8 to find the value at $\frac{1}{4}$; for as $\frac{1}{4}$ is an eighth part of 2 d., the value at $\frac{1}{4}$ must be an eighth part of the value at 2 d. The latter example is wrought in a similar manner.

		d.		L.	s.	d.
3.	3596 at	$2\frac{1}{4}$	Answer	33	14	3
4.	1861 at	$1\frac{1}{4}$	———	9	13	$10\frac{1}{4}$
5.	7000 at	$4\frac{1}{4}$	———	123	19	2
6.	7181 at	5	———	149	12	1
7.	3762 at	7	———	109	14	6
8.	3747 at	$7\frac{1}{2}$	———	117	1	$10\frac{1}{2}$
9.	4697 at	8	———	156	11	4
10.	7924 at	$9\frac{1}{2}$	———	313	13	2
11.	7796 at	$10\frac{1}{2}$	———	341	1	6
12.	3064 at	11	———	140	8	8

When the price is not less than a shilling, but less than two shillings, work by

RULE 4.

Set down the value of the given number at a shilling, and to this add the value at the rest of the price, found by the preceding rules.

EXAMPLES.

1. What is the value of 725 yards of muslin, at 13½ d. per yard?

1½	⅛	725 s.		value at 1 s.
		90	7½	value at 1½ d.

2|0)81|5 7½ Ans. in shillings, &c.

Ans. reduced 40 L. 15 s. 7½ d.

	d.		L.	s.	d.
2.	15 at 13½	Answer		16	10½
3.	360 at 14	———	21	0	0
4.	1479 at 15	———	92	8	9
5.	7121 at 16¼	———	482	3	0¼
6.	2340 at 17½	———	170	12	6
7.	7890 at 18¾	———	616	8	1½
8.	8900 at 19	———	704	11	8
9.	7120 at 20¼	———	600	15	0
10.	1376 at 21	———	120	8	0
11.	6812 at 22¾	———	645	14	5
12.	9999 at 23¾	———	989	9	8½

When the price is any number of shillings under 20, work by

RULE 5.

Set down the value of the given number at a shilling, and multiply that sum by the number of shillings in the price: the product will be the answer.* Or,

If the price be an aliquot part of a pound, set down the value of the given number at a pound, and take such part of that sum as the price is of a pound, for the answer.

EXAMPLES.

1. What is the value of 528 bu. of apples, at 3 s. per bu.?
2. What is the value of 750 yds. of linen, at 5 s. per yd.?

s.
528 value at 1 s.
3

2|0)158|4 Ans. in shillings.

Ans. 79 L. 4 s.

L.
| 5 s. | ¼ | 750 value at 1 L.

Ans. 187 L. 10 s.

* As two shillings are twice one shilling, the value of any number of articles, at two shillings, each, must be twice their value at one shilling; and as three shillings are three times one shilling, the value at three shillings must be three times the value at one shilling, &c.

							L.	s.	d.
			s.						
3.	264	at	3.	Answer			39	12	0
4.	486	at	2.	———			48	12	0
5.	121	at	5.	———			30	5	0
6.	1286	at	4.	———			257	4	0
7.	860	at	7.	———			301	0	0
8.	242	at	11.	———			133	2	0
9.	2798	at	13.	———			1818	14	0
10.	3679	at	17.	———			3127	3	0

Note.—When the price is an even number of shillings, the answer may be found thus:—Multiply the given number by half the price, doubling the right hand figure of the product for shillings; the rest of the product will be pounds.

11. 473 at 4 s. Ans. 94 L. 12 s.

473
2
———
Ans. 94 L. 12 s.

			s.		L.	s.	d.
12.	946	at	4.	Answer	189	4	0
13.	713	at	6.	———	213	18	0
14.	916	at	8.	———	366	8	0
15.	739	at	12.	———	443	8	0
16.	171	at	16.	———	136	16	0

When the price is shillings and pence, or shillings, pence, and farthings, work by

RULE 6.

If the price be an aliquot part of a pound, set down the value of the given number at a pound, and take such part of that value as the price is of a pound, for the answer: but,

If the price be not an aliquot part of a pound, find the value at the shillings, by rule 5; and to this add the value at the rest of the price, found by the preceding rules.

EXAMPLES.

1. 764 yards, at 2 s. 6d. Ans. 95 L. 10 s.

| 2 s. 6 d. | $\frac{1}{8}$ | 764 value at 1 L. (L.)
———
Ans. 95 L. 10 s.

2. 428 lb. at 5 s. 9 d. Ans. 123 L. 1 s.

		s.	
6 d.	½	428	value at 1 s.
		5	
		2140	value at 5 shillings.
3 d.	½	214	—— at 6 pence.
		107	—— at 3 pence.

2|0)246|1 Answer in shillings.

Ans. reduced 123 L. 1 s.

			s.	d.		L.	s.	d.
3.	378	at	1	8	Answer	31	10	0
4.	324	at	2	6	——	40	10	0
5.	126	at	3	4	——	21	0	0
6.	716	at	6	8	——	238	13	4
7.	673	at	5	10½	——	197	13	10½
8.	2547	at	7	3½	——	928	11	10½
9.	3715	at	9	4½	——	1741	8	1½
10.	2572	at	13	7½	——	1752	3	6
11.	7251	at	14	8¼	——	5324	19	0¾
12.	1924	at	19	6	——	1875	18	0
13.	2710	at	19	2½	——	2602	14	7

When the price is pounds, or pounds, shillings, &c., work by

RULE 7.

Set down the value of the given number at a pound, and multiply that sum by the number of pounds in the price: the product will be the value at the pounds, to which add the value at the remainder of the price (if any) found agreeably to the tenor of the preceding rules: or,

Reduce the pounds and shillings of the price to shillings, and find the answer by Rule 6.

EXAMPLES.

1. 428 tons, at 3 L. 4 s. $6\frac{1}{2}$ d. per ton.
Ans. 1381 L. 3 s. 10 d.

		L.
4 s.	$\frac{1}{5}$	428 value at 1 L.
		3
		1284
6d.	$\frac{1}{8}$	85 12
$\frac{1}{2}$	$\frac{1}{12}$	10 14
		17 10
Answer		1381 L. 3 s. 10 d.

Or thus :

		s.
6 d.	$\frac{1}{2}$	428
		64
		1712
		2568
		27392
$\frac{1}{2}$	$\frac{1}{12}$	214
		17 10
		2|0)2762|3 10

Ans. 1381 L. 3 s. 10 d.

			L.	s.	d.		L.	s.	d.
2.	47	at	3	3	4	Answer	148	16	8
3.	17	at	2	6	8	———	39	13	4
4.	17	at	11	14	0	———	198	18	0
5.	20	at	4	13	4	———	93	6	8
6.	71	at	6	13	4	———	473	6	8
7.	156	at	3	6	$8\frac{1}{4}$	———	520	3	3
8.	457	at	14	17	$9\frac{1}{2}$	———	6804	10	$9\frac{1}{2}$

When the given quantity consists of several denominations, and the price relates to the highest of those denominations, work by

RULE 8.

Multiply the price by the number of the highest denomination in the given quantity, and the product will be the value thereof; to which add the value of the remaining denominations, found by taking parts of the price : or,

Find the value of the number of the highest denomination by one of the preceding rules, to which add the value of the remaining denominations, found as before.

EXAMPLES.

1. What is the value of 171 cwt. 1 qr. 7 lb. of sugar, at 3 L. 6 s. 8 d. per cwt.? Ans. 571 L. 0 s. 10 d.

qr.		L.	s.	d.	
1	¼	3	6	8×1	
				10	
		33	6	8×7	
				10	
		333	6	8	value of 171 cwt.
		3	6	8	
lb.		233	6	8	
7	¼		16	8	value of 1 qr.
			4	2	value of 7 lb.

Ans. 571 L. 0 s. 10 d.

Or thus:

s. d.		L.
6 8	½	171
1qr.	¼	3
		513
		57
7lb.	¼	0 16 8
		4 2

Ans. 571 L. 0 s. 10d.

	cwt.	qrs.	lb.		L.	s.	d.			L.	s.	d.
2.	12	2	14	at	3	14	0	per cwt.	Ans.	46	14	3
3.	17	3	19	at	2	2	6	——	——	38	1	6¾
4.	10	0	12	at	1	19	6	——	——	19	19	2½
5.	9	2	26	at	4	10	4½	——	——	43	19	6
6.	5	1	0	at	2	17	0	——	——	14	19	3
7.	7	0	19	at	3	16	0	——	——	27	4	10½

	lbs.	oz.	dwt.		L.	s.	d.					
8.	27	10	0	at		1	4	per lb.	——	1	17	1¼
9.	73	5	15	at	3	9	0	——	——	253	10	0¾

	yds.	qrs.		s.	d.					
10.	67	2	at	12	2	per yard.	——	41	1	3
11.	68	1	at	8	1	——	——	27	11	8¼
12.	419	3	at	12	6	——	——	262	6	10½

	A.	R.	P.		L.	s.	d.					
13.	476	3	28	at	3	7	11	per acre.	——	1619	11	1¾
14.	238	1	34	at	6	15	10	——	——	1619	11	1¾

EXAMPLES IN FEDERAL MONEY.

Note.—When the given price of an article is in Federal money, the question may generally be answered by Multiplication, or by the Rule of Three, more readily than by Practice. It is useful, however, to be acquainted with the method of working by Practice, as it affords a means of proving the correctness of operations performed by those other rules.

The examples that are given in this place are chiefly confined to cases in which the price is an aliquot part of a dollar: for working which the following is a

GENERAL RULE.

Set down the value of the given number at a dollar, and take such part of that sum as the price is of a dollar, for the answer.

1. What is the value of 800 loaves of bread, at $6\frac{1}{4}$ cents each, and also at $12\frac{1}{2}$ cents each?

		dols.				*dols.*
$6\frac{1}{4}$	$\frac{1}{16}$	800 (50 dols. Ans.		$12\frac{1}{2}$	$\frac{1}{8}$	800 value at 1 dol.
		80				Ans. 100 dollars.
		0				

		Dols.cts.
2. 720 lb. of pork, at $6\frac{1}{4}$ cts. per lb.	Ans.	45.00
3. 1446 lb. of beef, at $6\frac{1}{4}$ cts. per lb.	—	$90.37\frac{1}{2}$
4. 680 lb. of sugar, at 10 cts. per lb.	—	68.00
5. 2128 lb. of cheese, at 10 cts. per lb.	—	212.80
6. 336 lb. of sugar, at $12\frac{1}{2}$ cts. per lb.	—	42.00
7. 1364 lb. of ham, at $12\frac{1}{2}$ cts. per lb.	—	170.50
8. 160 yds. of muslin, at 20 cts. per yd.	—	32.00
9. 1462 yds. of check, at 20 cts. per yd.	—	292.40
10. 240 lb. of coffee, at 25 cts. per lb.	—	60.00
11. 726 yds. of muslin, at 25 cts. per yd.	—	181.50
12. 324 yds. of linen, at 50 cts. per yd.	—	162.00
13. 75 bush. of potatoes, at 50 cts. per bu.	—	37.50

Note.—When the given quantity consists of several denominations, proceed as directed in Rule 8.

14. 2cwt. 3qrs. 14lbs. at $7.00 per cwt. Ans. $$20.12\frac{1}{2}$.

		dols.
		2
2 qrs.	$\frac{1}{2}$	7
		14
1 qr.	$\frac{1}{2}$	3.50
14 lb.	$\frac{1}{2}$	1.75
		$87\frac{1}{2}$
		Ans. $$20.12\frac{1}{2}$.

Or thus:

2 qrs.	$\frac{1}{2}$	7.00
		2
		14.00
1 qr.	$\frac{1}{2}$	3.50
14 lb.	$\frac{1}{2}$	1.75
		$87\frac{1}{2}$
		Ans. $$20.12\frac{1}{2}$.

15. 37 cwt. 2 qrs. 14 lb. at $20.10 per cwt.
Ans. $$756.26\frac{1}{4}$.

16. 7 cwt. 0 qrs. 16 lb. at $6.20 per cwt.
Ans. $$44.28\frac{1}{2}$.

17. 4 cwt. 1 qr. 16 lb. at $14.43 per cwt.
Ans. $63.38¾ +

18. 47 lb. 10 oz. (Troy Weight) at $1.25 per lb.
Ans. $59.79 +

19. 64 yds. 3 qrs. at $2.25 per yd. Ans. $145.68¾ +

20. 240 A. 1 R. 10 P. at $15.25 per acre.
Ans. $3664.76½.

APPLICATION.

1. What is the value of 120 lb. of rice, at 3d. per lb.?
Ans. 1 L. 10 s.

2. Bought 640 lb. of pork, at 4d. per lb.; what is the amount? Ans. 10 L. 13 s. 4 d.

3. How much will 3906 lb. of beef come to, at 7½d. per lb.? Ans. 122 L. 1 s. 3 d.

4. What is the amount of 2004 lb. of sugar, at 10½ d. per lb.? Ans. 87 L. 13 s. 6 d.

5. How much will 121 lb. of cheese come to, at 1 s. per lb.? Ans. 6 L. 1 s.

6. What is the value of 1234 yards of muslin, at 1 s. 11¾ d. per yard? Ans. 122 L. 2 s. 3½ d.

7. If 1 yard of linen cost 4 s., how much will 987 yards cost? Ans. 197 L. 8 s.

8. If 1 gallon of wine sell for 11 s., what will 543 gallons bring? Ans. 298 L. 13 s.

9. How much will 800 bushels of wheat amount to, at 13 s. 4 d. per bushel? Ans. 533 L. 6 s. 8 d.

10. How much will 47 tons of hay amount to, at 6 L. 6 s. 8 d. per ton? Ans. 297 L. 13 s. 4 d.

11. If 1 yard of cloth cost 1 L. 19 s. 4 d., how much will 1677 yards come to? Ans. 3298 L. 2 s.

12. Sold 3906 lb. of sugar, at 12½ cents per lb. what is the amount? Ans. 488 dols. 25 cts.

13. Bought 324 yards of calico, at 25 cents per yard; what is the amount? Ans. 81 dols.

14. What will 16 cwt. 2 qrs. 17 lbs. of sugar amount to, at 5 L. 11 s. 10 d. per cwt.? Ans. 93 L. 2 s. 2½ d.

15. Sold 83 yds. 2 qrs. of superfine cloth, at 10 dols. 50 cts. per yard; how much does it amount to?
Ans. 876.75.

16. If 1 acre of land be worth 11 L. 15 s., what is the value of 578 acres 3 roods? Ans. 6800 L. 6 s. 3 d.

TARE AND TRET.

Tare and Tret are allowances made by the seller to the buyer, on some particular commodities.

Tare is an allowance made for the weight of the barrel, box, bag, or whatever contains the commodity.

Tret is an allowance of 4 lb. in every 104 lb. for waste, dust, &c.

Gross weight is the weight of the goods, together with the barrel, box, bag, or whatever contains them.

Neat weight is the weight of the goods after all allowances are deducted.

CASE 1.

To find the neat weight when the tare is so much in the whole gross weight.

RULE.

Subtract the tare from the gross weight, and the remainder will be the neat weight.

EXAMPLES.

1. The gross weight of a certain hogshead of sugar is 7 cwt. 3 qrs. 16 lb.; the tare is 3 qrs. 10 lb.; what is the neat weight? Ans. 7 cwt. 0 qrs. 6 lb.

2. What is the neat weight of 12 hogsheads of sugar, the gross weight of each hogshead being 6 cwt. 2 qrs. 17 lb.; the tare in the whole 8 cwt. 3 qrs. 14 lb.? Ans. 70 cwt. 3 qrs. 22 lb.

(1)

	cwt.	*qrs.*	*lb.*	
	7	3	16	gross.
		3	10	tare.
Ans.	7	0	6	neat.

(2)

	cwt.	*qrs.*	*lb.*	
	6	2	17	gross, each.
			12	
	79	3	8	gross in all.
	8	3	14	tare in all.
Ans.	70	3	22	neat weight.

3. The gross weight of a certain hogshead of sugar is 8 cwt. 3 qrs. 17 lbs.; the tare is 3 qrs. 16 lb.; what is the neat weight? Ans. 8 cwt. 0 qrs. 1 lb.

4. What is the neat weight of 456 cwt. 1 qr. 19 lb. of tobacco, tare in the whole 15 cwt. 2 qrs. 13 lb.? Ans. 440 cwt. 3 qrs. 6 lb.

5. What is the neat weight of 4 casks of Indigo, the gross weight of each cask being 4 cwt. 2 qrs. 14 lb.; the tare in the whole 1 cwt. 0 qrs. 26 lb.?

Ans. 17 cwt. 1 qr. 2 lb.

6. What is the neat weight of 5 casks of sugar, the gross weight and tare as follows?

		cwt.	*qrs.*	*lb.*		*qrs.*	*lb.*
No. 1.	Gross	4	2	14	Tare	1	5
2.	——	3	0	17	——	1	1
3.	——	5	3	10	——	2	11
4.	——	6	1	16	——	2	27
5.	——	3	2	18	——	1	3

Ans. 21 cwt. 2 qrs.

CASE 2.

To find the neat weight when the tare is so much per barrel, box, &c.

RULE.

Multiply the tare per barrel, box, &c., by the number of barrels, boxes, &c., and the product will be the whole tare: subtract the whole tare from the whole gross weight, and the remainder will be the neat weight.

EXAMPLES.

1. What is the neat weight of 15 casks of raisins, each weighing 2 cwt. 3 qrs. 12 lb. gross—tare 21 lb. per cask?

cwt.	*qrs.*	*lb.*	
2	3	12	
		5	
14	1	4	
		3	
42	3	12	gross.
2	3	7	tare.
40	0	5	neat.

```
    15 casks.
    21 tare per cask.
    —
    15
   30
   ——
28)315 lb.(4)11 qrs.
   28         —
   ——           2 cwt. 3 qrs. 7 lb.
    35
    28
    —
     7
```

2. What is the neat weight of 4 hogsheads of tobacco, each weighing 10 cwt. 3 qrs. 10 lb. gross; tare 100 lb. per hhd.? Ans. 39 cwt. 3 qrs. 4 lb.

3. What is the neat weight of 6 casks of raisins, each weighing 3 cwt. 2 qrs. 10 lb. gross; tare 20 lb. per cask? Ans. 20 cwt. 1 qr. 24 lb.

4. What is the neat weight of 35 bales of silk, each weighing 317 lb. gross; tare 16 lb. per bale? Ans. 10535 lb.

CASE 3.

To find the neat weight when the tare is so much per hundred weight.

RULE.

Subtract from the gross such aliquot part or parts of it, as the tare is of a cwt.; the remainder will be the neat. Or, multiply the pounds gross by the tare per cwt., then divide the product by 112, and the quotient will be the tare. Subtract the tare from the pounds gross, and the remainder will be the neat weight.

EXAMPLES.

1. What is the neat weight of 40 kegs of figs, gross weight 75 cwt. 3 qrs. 12 lb.; tare per cwt. 14 lb.?

		cwt.	*qrs.*	*lb.*	
14	$\frac{1}{8}$	75	3	12	gross.
		9	1	26	tare.
		66	1	14	neat.

2. What is the neat weight of 35 kegs of raisins, gross weight 37 cwt. 1 qr. 20 lb.; tare per cwt. 14 lb.? Ans. 32 cwt. 3 qrs.

3. What is the neat weight of 6 hogsheads of sugar, each weighing 8 cwt. 2 qrs. 14 lb. gross; tare 16 lb. per cwt.? Ans. 44 cwt. 1 qr. 12 lb.

4. What is the neat weight of 9 hogsheads of tobacco, each weighing 6 cwt. 2 qrs. 12 lb. gross; tare 17 lb. per cwt.? Ans. 50 cwt. 1 qr. 22 lb.

CASE 4.

To find the neat weight when tret is allowed with tare.

RULE.

Subtract the tare from the gross weight as before: the

remainder is called suttle. Divide the suttle by 26, and the quotient will be tret. Subtract the tret from the suttle, and the remainder will be the neat weight.

EXAMPLES.

1. What is the neat weight of 8 cwt. 3 qrs. 20 lb. gross; tare 38 lb.; tret 4 lb. per 104 lb.?

```
Cwt. qrs. lb.
 8   3   20
 4                   Suttle 962
 —                  26)962(  37 tret.
35                     78    ——
28                     ——   925 lb. neat.
——                     182
300                    182
70                     ——
———
1000 lb. gross.
  38 lb. tare.
———
 962 lb. suttle.
```

2. What is the neat weight of 17 chests of sugar, weighing 120 cwt. 2 qrs. gross; tare 176 lb.; tret 4 lb. per 104 lb.? Ans. 12808 lb. or 114 cwt. 1 qr. 12 lb.

3. What is the neat weight of 5 hogsheads of sugar, each 10 cwt. 1 qr. 20 lb. gross; tare 3 qrs. 25 lb. per hhd.; tret 4 lb. per 104 lb.? Ans. 45 cwt. 1 qr. 24 lb.

APPLICATION.

1. There are 24 hogsheads of tobacco: each hogshead weighs 6 cwt. 2 qrs. 17 lb. gross; tare in all, 17 cwt. 3 qrs. 27 lb. How much will the tobacco amount to, at 1 L. 10 s. 6 d. per cwt.? Ans. 216 L. 0 s. 4½ d.

2. Bought 5 bags of coffee, each of which weighed 95 lb. gross; tare in the whole, 10 lb. How much did it amount to, at 25 cents per pound? Ans. $116.25.

3. What is the amount of 30 casks of raisins; each cask weighing 2 cwt. 3 qrs. 12 lb. gross; tare 21 lb. per cask; price, $7.35 per cwt.? Ans. $588.65½.

4. What is the value of 10 casks of alum; the whole weighing 33 cwt. 2 qrs. 15 lb. gross; tare 15 lb. per cask; price, 23 s. 4 d. per cwt.? Ans. 37 L. 13 s. 6½ d.

5. Sold 12 butts of currants; each butt weighed 7 cwt.

1 qr. 10 lb. gross; tare 16 lb. per cwt. What was the amount at $9.20 per cwt.? Ans. 694.51\frac{5}{7}$.

6. What is the value of 8 hogsheads of sugar, each weighing 8 cwt. 3 qrs. 7 lb.; tare 12 lb. per cwt.; price 72 s. 6 d. per cwt.? Ans. 228 L. 3 s. 7$\frac{1}{4}$ d.

SIMPLE INTEREST.

Interest is a consideration allowed for the use of money; relative to which are four particulars, viz., the principal, time, rate per cent., and amount.

The *principal*, is the money for which interest is to be received.

The *rate per cent.* per annum is the interest of 100 pounds or dollars for one year.

The *time* is the number of years or months, &c., for which interest is to be calculated.

The *amount* is the sum of the principal and interest.

CASE 1.

To find the interest when the time is one year, and the rate per cent. is pounds or dollars only.

RULE.*

Multiply the principal by the rate per cent., and divide the product by 100: the quotient will be the interest for 1 year.

PROOF.

By the Single Rule of Three.

EXAMPLES.

1. What is the interest of 525 L. for 1 year, at 6 L. per cent. per annum? Ans. 31 L. 10 s.

2. What is the interest of 650 L. 15 s. for 1 year, at 6 L. per cent. per annum?

* This rule agrees with the Single Rule of Three, except that the stating required by that rule is omitted in this.

(1)

```
     525
       6
   -----
L. 31|50
      20
   -----
s. 10|00
```

(2)

```
 L.     s.
650     15
         6
----------
39|04   10
   20
-----
 0|90
   12
-----
10|80
-----
 3|20
```

3. What is the interest of 500 L. for one year, at 6 L. per cent. per annum? Ans. 30 L.

4. What is the interest of 1000 L. for one year, at 7 L. per cent. per annum? Ans. 70 L.

5. What is the interest of 350 L. 17 s. 8 d. for one year, at 6 L. per cent. per annum? Ans. 21 L. 1 s. 0½ d.

6. What is the interest of 220 L. for one year, at 4 L. per cent. per annum? Ans. 8 L. 16 s.

7. What is the interest of 76 L. for one year, at 5 L. per cent. per annum? Ans. 3 L. 16 s.

8. What is the interest of 270 L. 10 s. 6 d. for one year, at 5 L. per cent. per annum? Ans. 13 L. 10 s. 6¼ d.

9. What is the interest of 542 dollars for one year, at 6 dollars per cent. per annum? Ans. $32.52.

```
   542
     6
------
$32.52
```

10. What is the interest of 756 dollars for one year, at 7 dollars per cent. per annum? Ans. $52.92.

11. What is the interest of 600 dollars for one year, at 5 dollars per cent. per annum? Ans. $30.00.

12. What is the interest of $438.25 for one year, at 6 dollars per cent. per annum?
Ans. 26 dols. 29 cts. 5 m. or $26.29½

```
 D.  cts.
438  25
      6
---------
26|29  50
   100
---------
  29|50
     10
  ------
   5|00
```

Or thus:

```
 D.   cts.
438   25
       6
----------
$26.29.5|0
```

13. What is the interest of $322.71 for one year, at 5 dollars per cent. per annum? Ans. $16.13½.

14. What is the interest of $75.95 for one year, at 7 dollars per cent. per annum? Ans. $5.31½+

Note.—When the amount is required, add the principal to the interest.

15. What is the amount of 173 L. 17 s. 8½ d. for one year, at 7 L. per cent. per annum?

Ans. 186 L. 1 s. 1¾ d.

16. What is the amount of a bond for 756 dollars, for one year, at 6 dollars per cent. per annum?

Ans. $801.36.

CASE 2.

When there is a fraction, as ¼, ½, ¾, &c., in the rate per cent.

RULE.

Multiply the principal by the pounds or dollars of the rate per cent.; to the product add ¼, ½, or ¾, &c., of said principal, and divide the result by 100, as in the foregoing case.

EXAMPLES.

1. What is the interest of 432 L. 10 s. for one year, at 5½ L. per cent. per annum?

Ans. 23 L. 15 s. 9 d.

2. What is the interest of 428 dollars for one year, at $6\frac{1}{4}$ dollars per cent. per annum?

Ans. $26.75.

(1)			(2)
	L.	s.	Dols.
$\frac{1}{2}$	432	10	$\frac{1}{4}$ | 428
		$5\frac{1}{2}$	$6\frac{1}{4}$
	2162	10	2568
	216	5	107
	23 | 78	15	$26.75
	20		
	15 | 75		
	12		
	9 | 00		

3. What is the interest of 216 L. 5 s. for one year, at $5\frac{1}{2}$ L. per cent. per annum?

Ans. 11 L. 17 s. $10\frac{1}{2}$ d.

4. What is the interest of 500 L. for one year, at $6\frac{1}{4}$ L. per cent. per annum? Ans. 31 L. 5 s.

5. What is the interest of 855 L. 17 s. 6 d. for one year, at $5\frac{3}{4}$ L. per cent. per annum?

Ans. 49 L. 4 s. 3 d.

6. What is the interest of 300 dollars for one year, at $6\frac{1}{4}$ dollars per cent. per annum?

Ans. $18.75.

CASE 3.

To find the interest when the time is two or more years.

RULE.

Find the interest of the given sum for one year: then multiply the interest for 1 year by the number of years given.

PROOF.

By the Double rule of Three.

EXAMPLES.

1. What is the interest of 700 L. 16 s. 8 d. for 5 years, at 6 L. per cent. per annum? Ans. 210 L. 5 s.

L.	s.	d.		L.	s.
700	16	8	Interest for 1 year	42	1
		6			5
42|05	0	0	Interest for 5 years	210	5
20					
1|00					

2. What is the interest of 750 L. for 3 years, at 6 L. per cent. per annum? Ans. 135 L.

3. What is the interest of 375 L. 10 s. 6 d. for 4 years, at 7 L. per cent. per annum? Ans. 105 L. 2 s. 11 d.

4. What is the interest of 353 L. 6 s. 3 d. for 9 years, at 5 L. per cent. per annum? Ans. 158 L. 19 s. 9¾ d.

5. What is the interest of $438.25 for 5 years, at 6 dollars per cent. per annum? Ans. $131.47½.

6. What is the interest of 1000 L. for 4 years, at 6¼ L. per cent. per annum? Ans. 250 L.

7. What is the interest of 1711 L. 15 s. for 2 years, at 5¾ L. per cent. per annum? Ans. 196 L. 17 s.

8. What is the interest of 320 dollars for 6 years, at 5½ dollars per cent. per annum? Ans. $105.60.

9. What is the amount of 720 L. for 3 years, at 6 L. per cent. per annum? Ans. 849 L. 12 s.

10. On a mortgage for 1256 dollars there is 4 years, interest due, at 6 dollars per cent. per annum, which is to be paid with the principal; what sum will discharge the debt? Ans. $1557.44

CASE 4.

To find the interest when the given time is months, weeks, or days, less or more than a year.

RULE.

Find the interest of the given sum for one year, then,

As one year
Is to the given time,
So is the interest of the given sum for one year,
To the interest required.

Or, take parts of the yearly interest for the aliquot

parts of a year that are in the given time, and add the interest for the odd days (if any) found by the Rule of Three.

EXAMPLES.

1. What is the interest of 350 L. for 3 years and 10 months, at 6 L. per cent. per annum? Ans. 80 L. 10 s.

```
     L.            Y.    Y.  M.      L.
    350            1  :  3   10  ::  21
      6           12    12           46
  ---------       ---   ---         ---
 L. 21 | 00       12    46          126
                                    84
                                   ----
                                 12)966
                                    80 I   10 s.
```

Or thus:

```
     M.         L.
   | 6 | 1/2 | 21 interest for one year.
   | 4 | 1/8 |  3
   |   |     | --
   |   |     | 63 interest for three years.
   |   |     | 10 10—— for six months.
   |   |     |  7 00—— for four months.
               -------
               80 L. 10 s.
```

2. What is the interest of 150 L. 19 s. for 3 years and 4 months, at 6 L. per cent. per annum? Ans. 30 L. 3 s. 9 d.

3. What is the interest of 57 L. 17 s. 8 d. for 3 months, at 6 L. per cent. per annum? Ans. 17 s. $4\frac{1}{4}$ d.

4. What is the interest of 7500 dollars for 4 months, at 7 dollars per cent. per annum? Ans. $175.00.

5. What is the interest of 400 L. for 1 week, at 5 L. per cent. per annum? Ans. 7 s. $8\frac{1}{4}$ d.+

6. What is the interest of 126 L. 12 s. for 16 weeks, at $4\frac{1}{2}$ per cent. per annum? Ans. 1 L. 15 s. $0\frac{1}{2}$ d.+

7. What is the interest of 250 L. for 73 days, at 7 L. per cent. per annum? Ans. 3 L. 10 s.

8. What is the interest of 500 L. for 146 days, at 6 L. per cent. per annum? Ans. 12 L.

9. What is the interest of 71 L. 3 s. $11\frac{1}{2}$ d. for 1 year,

5 months, and 25 days, at 6 L. per cent. per annum ?
Ans. 6 L. 6 s. 10 d.

10. What is the amount of a bond for 967 dollars, for 2 years and 4 months, at 6 per cent. per annum ?
Ans. 1102.38.

11. What is the amount of 100 L. for 18 months, at 8 per cent. per annum ? Ans. 12 L.

Note.—The answers to the following questions may be found by the concise method at the bottom of the page : but it is thought best that the learner should first obtain them by the preceding general rule.*

12. What is the interest of 900 L. for 8 months, at 6 L. per cent. per annum ? Ans. 36 L.

13. What is the interest of 450 L. for 4 months, at 7 L. per cent. per annum ? Ans. 10 L. 10 s.

14. What is the interest of 148 L. 12 s. $6\frac{1}{2}$ d. for 11 months, at 6 per cent. per annum ? Ans. 8 L. 3 s. $5\frac{3}{4}$ d.

15. What is the interest of 1260 dollars for 4 months, at 6 dollars per cent. per annum : and also at 7 per cent. per annum ?

Ans. { $25.20 interest at 6 per cent.
$29.40 interest at 7 per cent.

---

* The interest of any sum for any number of months, may be concisely found by the following method:

Multiply the principal by half the number of months, and divide the product by 100 ; or multiply the principal by the whole number of months, divide the product by 2, and divide the quotient by 100: the result of either operation will be the interest at 6 per cent. per annum.

For the interest at any other rate per cent. take aliquot parts of the interest at 6 per cent., and add or subtract as the case requires.

EXAMPLE.

What is the interest of 450 L. for 8 months, at 6 L. per cent. per annum ; and also at 7 L. per cent. per annum ?

	Or thus:		
L.	*L.*		*L.*
450	450	$\frac{1}{6}$	18 interest at 6 per cent.
4	8		3 interest at 1 per cent.
18|00	2)3600		21 interest at 7 per cent.
	18|00		

16. What is the interest of 630 dollars for 8 months, at 6 dollars per cent. per annum? Ans. $25.20.

17. What is the interest of 7342 dollars for 16 months, at 6 dollars per cent. per annum? Ans. $587.36.

18. What is the interest of 750 dollars for 9 months, at 7 dollars per cent. per annum? Ans. $39.37½.

19. What is the interest of 375 dollars for 5½ months, at 6 dollars per cent. per annum? Ans. $10.31¼.

* 20. What is the interest of $460.50 for 4 months, at 6 dollars per cent. per annum? Ans. $9.21.

21. What is the interest of $230.25 for 8 months, at 7 dollars per cent. per annum? Ans. $10.74½.

22. What is the interest of $764.50 for 3 years and 10 months, at 6 dollars per cent. per annum?

Ans. $175.83½.

To find the interest of any given sum as computed at the banks, at 6 per cent.

RULE.

1. Multiply the dollars by the number of days, and divide the product by 6; the quotient will be the interest in mills. Or,

2. If the principal be any number of dollars, the interest for 60 days, at 6 per cent., will be exactly that

---

* When the principal consists of dollars and cents, the interest may be found thus:

Reduce the principal to cents, by removing the separating point: then multiply and divide as directed in the last note, and separate one figure from the right of the result as a remainder or fraction; the figures on the left of this will be the interest *in mills.*

EXAMPLE.

What is the interest of $425.98 for 3 months, at 6 dollars per cent. per annum? and also at 7 dollars per cent. per annum?

cts.		*D.cts.m.*
42598	$\frac{1}{6}$	6.38.9 int. at 6 p. ct.
3		1.06.4+int. at 1 p. ct.
2)127794		$7.45.3+int. at 7 p. ct.
Interest in mills 6389|7		

number of cents: and for the time more or less than 60, take aliquot parts.*

EXAMPLES.

1. What is the interest of 1542 dollars for 90 days, at 6 per cent. per annum? also, for 60,† for 30, and for 20 days, at the same rate?

Dols.			
1542	30	$\frac{1}{2}$	1542 int. for 60 days in cents.
90	20	$\frac{1}{3}$	771 int. for 30 days in cents.
6)138780			514 int. for 20 days in cents.
23130 mills.			

		D.	*cts.*
	Or, int. for 60 days	15	. 42.
Or, $23.13 int. for 90 days.	for 30 ——	7	. 71.
	for 20 ——	5	. 14.

2. What is the interest of 771 dollars for 90 days, at 6 per cent. per annum? Ans. $11.56½.

3. What is the interest of 3084 dollars for 30 days, at 6 per cent. per annum? Ans. $15.42.

4. What is the interest of 2324 dollars for 54 days, at 6 per cent. per annum? Ans. $20.91½+.

5. What is the interest of 3942 dollars for 50 days, at 6 per cent. per annum? Ans. $32.85.

CASE 5.

To find the principal, when the amount, time, and rate per cent. are given.

RULE.

Find the amount of 100 pounds, or dollars, at the rate and time given: then,

As the amount of 100 pounds, or dollars,
Is to the amount given,
So are 100 pounds, or dollars,
To the principal required.

---

* This is calculating after the rate of 360 instead of 365 days to the year, which will always make the interest rather too much.

If the interest found by this rule be divided by 73, the quotient will show by how much it exceeds the true interest.

† When a note is drawn for 60 days, the interest is mostly calculated for 63, on account of three days called days of grace, which are commonly allowed the payer, on all notes, after the time expires for which they are drawn. The interest is here only computed for the given time.

EXAMPLES.

1. What principal at interest for five years, at 6 per cent. per annum, will amount to 650 L.? Ans. 500 L.

```
L.                                    L.     L.       L.
6                                     130 : 650  ::  100
5 years                                     100
—                                         ———      L.
30 int. of 100 L. for 5 years.       130)65000(500
100                                        650
—                                         ———
130 amt. of 100 L. for 5 years.              00
```

2. What principal at interest for 10 years, at 6 per cent. per annum, will amount to 1300 L.?

Ans. 812 L. 10 s.

3. What principal at interest for 4 years, at 5 per cent. per annum, will amount to $571.20?

Ans. 476 dollars.

CASE 6.

To find the rate per cent. when the amount, time, and principal are given.

RULE.

Subtract the principal from the amount, and the remainder will be the interest for the given time: then,

As the principal,
Is to one hundred pounds or dollars,
So is the interest of the principal, for the given time,
To the interest of 100 pounds, or dollars, for the same time:

Again,
As the given time,
Is to one year,
So is the interest last found,
To the rate per cent. required.

EXAMPLES.

1. At what rate per cent. per annum, will 500 L. amount to 650 L. in 5 years? Ans. 6 L. per cent.

```
                             L.     L.      L.    L.
650 Amount.                 500 : 100 :: 150 : 30
500 Principal.                 again,
—                                Y.   Y.    L.    L.
150 Int. for the given time.     5 :  1 ::  30 :  6
```

2. At what rate per cent. per annum, will 500 L. amount to 725 L. in 9 years? Ans. 5 L. per cent.

3. At what rate per cent. per annum, will 600 dollars amount to 856 dols. 50 cts. in 9 years and 6 months? Ans. $4\frac{1}{2}$ per cent.

CASE 7.

To find the time, when the principal, amount, and rate per cent. are given.

RULE.

Find the interest of the principal for one year.

Find the interest for the time required, by subtracting the principal from the amount: then,

As the interest of the principal for one year,
Is to the interest for the time required,
So is one year,
To the time required.

EXAMPLES.

1. In what time will 500 L. amount to 725 L., at 5 per cent. per annum? Ans. 9 years.

L.	*L.*	*L.* *L.* *Y.* *Y.*
500	725	25 : 225 : : 1 : 9
5	500	
L. 25|00	225 Interest for the time required.	

2. In what time will 540 L. amount to 734 L. 8 s., at 4 per cent. per annum? Ans. 9 years.

3. In what time will 600 dollars amount to 798 dollars, at 6 per cent. per annum? Ans. $5\frac{1}{2}$ years.

INSURANCE, COMMISSION, AND BROKAGE.

Insurance, Commission, and Brokage, are allowances made to insurers, factors, and brokers, at a stipulated rate per cent.

RULE.

Work as if to find the interest of the given sum for one year, at the proposed rate: or, if the rate be less than 1 per cent., take such aliquot part or parts of the interest at 1 per cent. as the rate is of a pound, or dollar.

EXAMPLES.

1. What is the commission on 596 L. 18 s. 4 d., at 6 per cent.? Ans. 35 L. 16 s. $3\frac{1}{2}$ d.

```
        L.   s.  d.
       596  18   4
                 6
    -------------
 L. 35|81   10   0
       20
    -----
 s. 16|30
       12
    -----
  d. 3|60
        4
    -----
 qr. 2|40
```

2. What is the commission on 1371 L. 9 s. 5 d., at 5 per cent.? Ans. 68 L. 11 s. $5\frac{1}{2}$ d.

3. What is the commission on 526 L. 11 s. 5 d., at $3\frac{1}{2}$ L. per cent.? Ans. 18 L. 8 s. 7 d.

4. What is the commission on 1974 dollars, at 5 dollars per cent.? Ans. $98.70.

5. A factor has sold goods for a merchant to the amount of 930 L. 10 s., and is to receive $3\frac{1}{4}$ L. per cent. commission: what sum is due to him?
Ans. 30 L. 4 s. $9\frac{3}{4}$ d.

6. What is the insurance of 924 L., at 7 L. per cent.?
Ans. 64 L. 13 s. 7 d.

7. What is the insurance of 1250 dollars, at $7\frac{1}{2}$ dollars per cent.? Ans. $93.75.

8. What is the insurance of an East India ship and cargo, valued at 14813 L. 15 s., at $15\frac{3}{4}$ L. per cent.?
Ans. 2333 L. 3 s. $3\frac{3}{4}$ d.

9. What is the brokage on 1321 L. 11 s. 4 d., at $1\frac{1}{8}$ L. per cent.? Ans. 14 L. 17 s. 4 d.

10. What is the brokage on 874 L. 15 s. 3 d., at 5 s. or $\frac{1}{4}$ L. per cent.? Ans. 2 L. 3 s. $8\frac{3}{4}$ d.

11. If a broker buy goods for me to the amount of $1853, and I allow him $\frac{3}{4}$ dollars per cent. for his service, what sum must I pay him? Ans. $13.89½.

COMPOUND INTEREST.

Compound Interest is that which arises from a principal increased by its interest, as the interest becomes due.

RULE.

Find the amount of the given principal for the first year, by simple interest; this amount will be the principal for the second year, and the amount of this principal, found as before, will be the principal for the third year, and so on.

From the last amount, subtract the given principal, and the remainder will be the compound interest.

EXAMPLES.

1. What is the compound interest of 500 L. for 3 years, at 5 per cent.? Ans. 78 L. 16 s. 3 d.

	L.		
Principal	500		
Interest for 1st year	25		
Amount 1st year	525		
Interest 2d year	26	5	
Amount 2d year	551	5	
Interest 3d year	27	11	3
Amount 3d year	578	16	3
Principal	500		
	L. 78	16 s.	3 d.

2. What is the compound interest of 450 L. for 3 years, at 5 per cent. per annum? Ans. 70 L. 18 s. 7½ d.

3. What is the compound interest of 760 L. 10 s. for 4 years, at 6 per cent. per annum?

Ans. 199 L. 12 s. 2 d.

4. What is the compound interest of 500 dollars for 4 years, at 6 per cent. per annum? Ans. 131.23\frac{3}{4}$.

5. How much will 400 L. amount to in 4 years, at 6 per cent. per annum? Ans. 504 L. 19 s. 9$\frac{1}{4}$ d.

DISCOUNT.

Discount is an allowance made for the payment of a sum of money before it becomes due, according to a certain rate per cent. agreed on between the parties concerned.

The present worth of any debt, not yet due, is so much money as, being put to interest, at a given rate per cent., till the debt become payable, will amount to a sum equal to the debt.

RULE.

Find the amount of 100 pounds, or dollars, at the rate and time given: then,

As the amount of 100 pounds, or dollars,
Is to the given sum, or debt,
So is 100 pounds, or dollars,
To the present worth.

Subtract the present worth from the debt, and the remainder will be the discount.

PROOF.

Find the amount of the present worth for the time and rate proposed, which must equal the given sum or debt.

EXAMPLES.

1. What is the present worth of 590 dollars, due in 3 years, discount at 6 per cent. per annum?

Ans. 500 dollars.

```
                          $     $       $
  $6 rate.               118 : 590 :: 100
   3 years.                    100
  ---                          ---
  18                      118)59000(500 dols.
  100                          590
  ---                          ---
  118 amt. of $100.             00.
```

2. What is the discount of 795 L. 11 s. 2 d. for 11 months, at 6 per cent. per annum? Ans. 41 L. 9 s. 6 d.

M.	*M*	*L.*	*L. s.*	*L. s. d.*	
12 :	11 : :	6 :	5 10	795 11 2	whole debt.
			100 0	754 1 8	present worth.
Amt. of 100 L.			105 10	41 9 6	discount.

L. s. *L. s. d.* *L.* *L. s. d.*
105 10 : 795 11 2 : : 100 : 754 1 8 present worth.

3. What is the present worth of 672 L. due in 2 years; discount at 6 per cent. per annum? Ans. 600 L.

4. What is the present worth of 308 L. 15 s. due in 18 months; discount at 8 per cent. per annum?
Ans. 275 L. 13 s. 4½ d.

5. What is the present worth of $430.67 due in 19 months; discount at 5 per cent. per annum?
Ans. $399.07.

6. What is the discount of 112 L. 12 s. due in 20 months, at 7 per cent. per annum? Ans. 11 L. 15 s. 3½ d.

7. What is the present worth of 100 L., one half due in 4 months, and the other half in 8 months; discount at 5 per cent. per annum? Ans. 97 L. 11 s. 4 d.

8. Bought goods amounting to $615.75, at 6 months' credit; how much ready money must be paid, if a discount of 4½ per cent. per annum be allowed?
Ans. $602.20.

9. What is the difference between the interest of 1204 dollars, at 5 per cent. per annum for 8 years; and the discount of the same sum for the same time and rate per cent.? Ans. $137.60.

Note.—Discount for present payment is often made without regard to time; it is then found precisely as the interest of the given sum for 1 year.

EXAMPLES.

1. How much is the discount of 853 dollars, at 2 per cent.? Ans. $17.06.

$$\begin{array}{r} 853 \\ 2 \\ \hline 17.06 \end{array}$$

2. How much is the discount of 750 dollars, at 3 per cent.? Ans. $22.50.

3. How much is the discount of 650 L., at 4 per cent.? Ans. 26 L.

4. Bought goods on credit, amounting to 1656 dollars; how much ready money must be paid for them, if a discount of 5 per cent. be allowed? Ans. \$1573.20.

5. A holds B's note for 175 L. 10 s.; he agrees to allow B a discount of 3 per cent. for present payment: what sum must B pay? Ans. 170 L. 4 s. $8\frac{1}{2}$ d.

EQUATION.

Equation is a method of reducing several stated times, at which money is payable, to one mean or equated time.

RULE.

Multiply each payment by its time, add the several products together, and divide the sum by the whole debt; the quotient will be the equated time.

PROOF.

The interest of the sum payable at the equated time, at any given rate, will equal the interest of the several payments, for their respective times, at the same rate.

EXAMPLES.

1. C owes D 100 dollars, of which 50 dollars is to be paid at 2 months, and 50 at 4 months; but they agree that the whole shall be paid at one time; when must it be paid? Ans. 3 months.

$$50 \times 2 = 100$$
$$50 \times 4 = 200$$

1 | 00) 3 | 00

3 months.

2. A owes B 380 L., of which 100 L. is to be paid at 6 months, 120 L. at 7 months, and 160 L. at 10 months, but they agree that the whole shall be paid at one time: when must it be paid? Ans. at 8 months.

3. A merchant has owing to him 300 L. to be paid as

follows: 50 L. at 2 months, 100 L. at 5 months, and 150 L. at 8 months; it is agreed to make one payment of the whole: at what time must it be paid? Ans. 6 months.

4. F owes H 2400 dollars, of which 480 dollars are to be paid at present, 960 dollars at 5 months, and the rest at 10 months, but they agree to make one payment of the whole, and wish to know the time.

Ans. 6 months.

5. A merchant has purchased goods to the amount of 2000 dollars, of which sum 400 dollars are to be paid at present, 800 dollars at 6 months, and the rest at 9 months; but it is agreed to make one payment of the whole: what is the equated time? Ans. 6 months.

6. G owes K 420 L., which will be due 6 months hence: it is agreed that 60 L. shall be paid now, and that the rest remain unpaid a longer time than 6 months: when must it be paid? Ans. in 7 months.

BARTER.

Barter is the exchanging of one commodity for another, according to the price or value agreed upon by the parties concerned.

Questions relating to Barter are solved either by the Rule of Three or by Practice.

Note.—When a given quantity of any commodity at a given price is to be bartered for another commodity at a given price, find the value, in money, of that commodity whose quantity is given; then find what quantity of the other may be had for that value.

EXAMPLES.

1. How much sugar, at 11 d. per lb., must be given in barter for 1100 lb. of rice, at $3\frac{1}{2}$ d. per lb.? Ans. 350 lb.

	d.		*d.*		*lb.*		*lb.*
1100	11	:	3850	::	1	:	350
$3\frac{1}{2}$							
3300							
550							
3850 d. the value of the rice.							

2. How much sugar, at 9 d. per lb., must be given in barter for 492 lb. of rice, at 3 d. per lb.? Ans. 164 lb.

3. How much tea, at 64 cents per lb., must be given in barter for 448 lb. of coffee, at 20 cts. per lb.? Ans. 140 lb.

4. What quantity of tea, at 10 s. per lb., must be given for 720 lb. of chocolate, at 4 s. 2 d. per lb.? Ans. 300 lb.

5. How much wheat, at 1 dol. 25 cts. per bushel, is equal in value to 50 bushels of rye, at 70 cents per bushel? Ans. 28 bushels.

6. B has 75 yards of muslin, at 1 s. 4 d. per yard, which he is to give to H for linen, at 5 s. per yard: how much linen will he receive? Ans. 20 yards.

7. A has sugar at 9 d. per lb., for a quantity of which F is to give him 225 lb. of tea, at 6 s. per lb.: how much sugar must F receive for his tea? Ans. 1800 lb.

8. How much sugar, at 8 d. per lb., must be given in barter for 20 cwt. of tobacco, at 3 L. per cwt.? Ans. 16 cwt. 0 qrs. 8 lb.

9. A merchant has 1000 yards of canvas, at $9\frac{1}{2}$ d. per yard, which he is to barter for serge, at $10\frac{1}{4}$ d. per yard: how many yards of serge should he receive? Ans. $926\frac{34}{41}$ yards.

10. A grocer bartered 5 cwt. of sugar, at 6 d. per lb., for cinnamon, at 10 s. 8 d. per lb.: how much cinnamon did he receive? Ans. 26 lb. 4 oz.

11. A has 41 cwt. of hops, at 30 s. per cwt., for which B is to give him 20 L. in money, and the rest in prunes, at 5 d. per lb.: what quantity of prunes must A receive? Ans 1992 lb.

12. A and B. barter: A has 320 lb. of chocolate, at 4 s. 6 d. per lb., for which B. is to give him 30 L. in money, and the rest in cotton, at 8 d. per lb.: how much cotton is B to give A? Ans. 1260 lb.

13. L has 41 cwt. of hops, at 4 dols. 50 cts. per cwt., for which M is to give him 28 dols. 50 cts. in money, and the rest in salt, at 80 cts. per bushel: what quantity of salt is M to give L? Ans. 195 bushels.

14. G has $28\frac{1}{2}$ lb. of tea, at 11 s. 6 d. per lb., for which B is to give him 40 yards of linen, at 7 s. 4 d. per yard, and the rest in money: how much money must G receive? Ans. 1 L. 14 s. 5 d.

15. R gave 189 yards of linen, at 6 s. 8 d. per yard, to C, for 42 yards of cloth; what was the cloth per yard? Ans. 30 s.

16. A has 608 yards of cloth, at 14 s. per yard, for which B is to give him 125 L. 12 s. in money, and 85 cwt. 2 qrs. 24 lb. of bees-wax. At how much is the bees-wax valued per cwt.? Ans. 3 L. 10 s.

17. C has wheat at $1.25 cents per bushel, ready money; but in barter he will have $1.50 per bushel: D has cotton at 20 cents per lb., ready money: what price must the cotton be in barter, and how much cotton must be given for 100 bushels of wheat?

Ans. { The cotton must be 24 cts. per lb., and 625 lb. must be given for 100 bushels of wheat

LOSS AND GAIN.

Loss and Gain instructs merchants and traders, so to estimate their goods in buying and selling, as to know what they gain or lose in dealing.

Questions in Loss and Gain are solved by the Rule of Three, or by Practice.

EXAMPLES.

1. A storekeeper sold 100 yards of silk, at $1.50 per yard, which cost him $1.25 per yard; how much did he gain by the sale?

$1.50
$1.25
———
25 gain per yard.

yd.   *yd's.*   *cts.*
1 : 100 : : 25
100
———
Whole gain $25.00

2. If a grocer buy 265 lb. of tea for 79 L. 10 s., and afterwards sell the whole at 7 s. per lb., how much will he gain by the transaction?

265
7
———
2|0)185|5
———
92 L. 15 s.

	L.	*s.*
Sold for	92	15
Cost	79	10
Gain L.	13	5

3. A shopkeeper bought 53 yards of silk, at 12 s. per yard, and afterwards sold it at 14 s. per yard; how much did he gain by the sale? Ans. 5 L. 6 s.

4. G bought 650 lb. of sugar, at 10 cents per lb., and sold it at 12 cents per lb.; how much did he gain? Ans. $13.00.

5. If I buy 765 yards of baize, at 3 s. $4\frac{1}{4}$ d. per yard, and sell it at 3 s. 9 d. per yard, how much do I gain? Ans. 14 L 6 s. $10\frac{1}{2}$ d.

6. Bought 2016 lb. of rice, at 3 d. per lb., and sold it at $3\frac{1}{2}$ d. per lb.: how much was gained by the transaction? Ans. 4 L. 4 s.

7. If I lay out 1000 dollars in hats, at 4 dollars each, and sell them afterwards at 4 dols. 50 cts. each, how much will I gain? Ans. $125.

8. A merchant bought 1300 lb. of coffee, at 22 cents per lb., and was afterwards obliged to sell it at 20 cents per lb.; how much did he lose? Ans. $26.00.

9. B laid out 250 L. in cloth, at 30 s. per yard, and, afterwards, finding it was damaged, sold it at 26 s. 3 d. per yard; how much did he lose? Ans. 31 L. 5 s.

10. A shopkeeper bought 42 yards of muslin for 4 L. 14 s. 8 d., and sold it at 2 s. 6 d. per yard; whether did he gain or lose, and how much? Ans. He gained 10 s. 4 d.

11. A draper bought 100 yards of cloth for 56 dollars: how must he sell it per yard, to gain 19 dollars in the whole? Ans. 75 cents.

12. If a grocer buy a quantity of tea for 125 L., and sell it again for 150 L., how much will he gain per cent.? Ans. 20 per cent.

13. If a yard of mantua be purchased for $1.20, and sold again for $1.50, what is the gain per cent.? Ans. 25 per cent.

14. If a yard of velvet be bought for 16 s., and sold again for 12 s., what is the loss per cent.? Ans. 25 per cent.

15. Bought a chest of tea, weighing 490 lb., for 326 dollars, and sold it for $370.10, what was the profit on each lb.? Ans. 9 cents.

16. If I buy 100 yards of cambric for 56 L., at how much must I sell it per yard, to gain 15 per cent.? Ans. 12 s. $10\frac{1}{2}$ d.

17. Bought 12 pieces of white cloth, for 6 L. 10 s. per piece, and paid 20 s. 10 d. per piece for dying it; how much must each piece be sold for, to gain 20 per cent.? Ans. 9 L. 1 s.

18. If a trader gain $1\frac{1}{2}$ d. per shilling on his goods, how much does he gain per cent.? Ans. $12\frac{1}{2}$ per ct.

19. If I buy 28 pieces of stuffs at 4 L. per piece, and sell 10 of the pieces at 6 L. per piece, and 8 at 5 L. per piece; at what rate per piece must I sell the rest, to gain 20 per cent. by the whole? Ans. 3 L. 8 s. $9\frac{1}{2}$ d.

20. Having bought a parcel of goods for 18 L., and sold the same immediately for 25 L., with 4 months credit, what is gained per cent. per annum?

Ans. 116 L. 13 s. $3\frac{3}{4}$ d.

FELLOWSHIP.

Fellowship is a rule, by which merchants, &c. trading in company with a joint stock, are enabled to ascertain each person's particular share of the gain or loss, in proportion to his share in the joint stock.

By this rule, also, legacies are adjusted, and the effects of bankrupts divided, &c.

CASE 1.

When the several stocks in company are considered without regard to time.

RULE.

As the whole sum, or stock,
Is to either person's share in stock, &c.
So is the whole gain or loss,
To that person's share of the gain or loss.

PROOF.

The sum of the several shares must equal the whole gain or loss.

EXAMPLES.

1. Three merchants, trading together, gained 800 dollars; A's stock was 1200 dols., B's 4800 dols., and C's 2000 dols. · what was each man's share of the gain?

A's stock 1200 dols.
B's stock 4800 dols.
C's stock 2000 dols.

Whole stock 8000 dollars.

As 8000 : 1200 : : 800 : 120 A's share of gain.
As 8000 : 4800 : : 800 : 480 B's share of gain.
As 8000 : 2000 : : 800 : 200 C's share of gain.

2. D, E, and F, trading together, gained 120 L.; D's stock was 140 L., E's was 300 L., and F's was 160 L.: what was each man's share of the gain?

Ans. D's share was 28 L., E's 60 L., F's 32 L.

3. Three merchants, trading together, lost goods to the value of 1920 dols.; now suppose A's stock was 2880 dols., B's 11520 dols., and C's 4800 dols.: what share of the loss must each man sustain?

Ans. { A's share 288 dols.
B's - 1152 dols.
C's - 480 dols.

4. A, B, and C freighted a ship with 108 tuns of wine, of which A had 48 tuns, B 36, and C 24, but by reason of stormy weather were obliged to cast 45 tuns overboard; how much must each man sustain of the loss?

Ans. A 20 tuns, B 15, and C 10.

5. If the money and effects of a bankrupt amount to 1400 L. 14 s. 6 d., and he is indebted to M 742 L. 12 s., to B 641 L. 19 s. 8 d., and to C 987 L. 19 s. 9 d.; how must the property be divided among them?

Ans. { M must have 438 L. 8 s. $4\frac{1}{4}$ d.
B - - - 379 L. 0 s. $3\frac{3}{4}$ d.
C - - - 583 L. 5 s. $9\frac{3}{4}$ d.

6. Suppose a person is indebted to S 70 L., to T 400 L., and to V 140 L. 12 s. 6 d., but upon his decease his property is found to be worth only 409 L. 14 s.; how must it be divided among his creditors?

Ans. { S must have 46 L. 19 s. $3\frac{3}{4}$ d.
T - - 268 L. 7 s. $7\frac{1}{4}$ d.
V - - 94 L. 7 s. $0\frac{1}{2}$ d.

7. Three graziers pay among them 120 dols. for a grass enclosure, into which they put 300 oxen, whereof L had 80, N 100, and C 120; how much should each person pay? Ans. L 32 dols., N 40 dols., and C 48 dols.

CASE 2.

When the respective stocks in company are considered with time.

RULE.

Multiply each man's stock by its time; then,

As the sum of the products,
Is to either particular product;
So is the whole gain or loss,
To the gain or loss of the stock from which that product is obtained.

EXAMPLES.

1. Three merchants traded together; A put in 120 L. for 9 months, B 100 L. for 16 months, and C 100 L. for 14 months, and they gained 100 L.; what is each man's share?

	L.		*m.*	
A's stock	120 ×	9 =	1080	
B's stock	100 ×	16 =	1600	
C's stock	100 ×	14 =	1400	
		Sum	4080	

Sum	*Prod.*	*L.*	*L. s. d.*	
As 4080 :	1080 : :	100 :	26 9 $4\frac{4}{5}$ +	A's share.
As 4080 :	1600 : :	100 :	39 4 $3\frac{3}{4}$ +	B's share.
As 4080 :	1400 : :	100 :	34 6 $3\frac{1}{4}$ +	C's share.

2. B, C, and D traded together; B put in 50 dollars for 4 months, C 100 dollars for 6 months, and D 150 dollars for 8 months; they gained $126.80: what is each man's share of the gain?

Ans. B's share is $12.68, C's $38.4, D's $76.8.

3. B and C trade in company; B put in 950 L. for 5 months, and C 785 L. for 6 months, and by trading they gain 275 L. 18 s. 4 d.; what is each man's share of the gain? Ans. B's 138 L. 10 s. 10 d., C's 137 L. 7 s. 6 d.

4. Three merchants trade in company; A put in 400 L. for 9 months, B 680 L. for 5 months, and C 120 L. for 12 months; but by misfortunes lost goods to the value of 500 L.: what must each man sustain of the loss?

Ans. { A must lose 213 L. 5 s. $4\frac{3}{4}$ d. +
B - - - 201 L. 8 s. 5 d. +
C - - - 85 L. 6 s. $1\frac{3}{4}$ d. + }

5. A, B, and C made a stock for 12 months; A put in at first $873.60, and 4 months after he put in $96.00 more; B put in at first $979.20, and at the end of 7 months he took out $206.40; C put in at first $355.20, and 3 months after he put in $206.40, and 5 months after that he put in $240.00 more. At the end of 12

months their gain is found to be $3446.40 : what is each man's share of the gain?

Ans. { A's share is $1334.82½
B's - - $1271.61½+
C's - - £839.96 }

EXCHANGE.

Exchange is the reduction of the money of one state or country to that of another.

Par is equality in value;* but the course of exchange is frequently above or below par.

Agio is a term used to signify the difference, in some countries, between bank and current money.

DOMESTIC EXCHANGE.

To change the currency of either state into that of any other, work by the Rule of Three; or by the theorems in the following page.

EXAMPLES.

1. What is the value of 750 L. Massachusetts currency in New York? Ans. 1000 L.

```
 s.   L.    s.              Or thus:
 6 : 750 : 8                  L.
      20                    3)750
   ------                     250
   15000                    -----
       8                    1000 L.
   ------
 6)120000
   ------
2|0)2000|0
   ------
   1000 L.
```

* *Note.*—A Spanish dollar is valued at 4 s. 6 d. sterling, and at 7 s. 6 d. Pennsylvania currency: 4 s. 6 d. sterling is therefore equal to 7 s. 6 d. Pennsylvania currency, and 100 L. of the former is equal to 166⅔ L. of the latter. When exchange between England and Pennsylvania is at this rate, it is said to be at par.

A TABLE,

Exhibiting the value of a dollar in each of the United States; and practical theorems for exchanging the currency of either into that of any other.

To exchange from / to	*New England States and Virginia.*	*Pennsylvania, Jersey, Delaw. and Maryland.*	*New York and N. Carolina.*	*S. Carolina and Georgia.*
* New England States and Virginia	Dollar 6 *s.* 0 *d.*	Add one 4th.	Add one 3d.	Subtract $\frac{1}{9}$ twice.
Pennsylvania, N. Jersey, Delaware, and Maryland.	Subtract one fifth.	Dollar 7 *s.* 6 *d.*	Add one 15th.	$\times 3\frac{1}{9}$ & $\div 5$.
New York and North Carolina.	Subtract one fourth.	Subtract one 16th.	Dollar 8 *s.* 0 *d.*	Multiply by 7 and divide by 12.
South Carolina and Georgia.	Add two 7ths.	Add $\frac{1}{2}$, $\frac{1}{7}$ that $\frac{1}{2}$ and $\frac{1}{2}$ that $\frac{1}{7}$.	Multiply by 12 and divide by 7.	Dollar 4 *s.* 8 *d.*

The New England States are, New Hampshire, Vermont, Massachusetts, Rhode Island, and Connecticut.

Note.—The value of a dollar in any state is found, either opposite to that state, or under it, in the table.

2. What is the value of 1500 L., Massachusetts currency, in New York? Ans. 2000 L.

3. What is the value of 240 L., Pennsylvania currency, in New York? Ans. 256 L.

4. What is the value of 933 L. 6 s. 8 d., South Carolina currency, in Pennsylvania? Ans. 1500 L.

5. What sum in Pennsylvania currency is equal to 120 L. 10 s. in New York? Ans. 112 L. 19 s. $4\frac{1}{2}$ d.

6. What sum in Pennsylvania currency is equal to 234 L. 4 s. in New England or Virginia?

Ans. 292 L. 15 s.

7. What is the value of 173 L. 16 s., New Jersey currency, in New York? Ans. 185 L. 7 s. $8\frac{3}{4}$ d.

8. What is the value of 900 L., New England or Virginia currency, in South Carolina? Ans. 700 L.

9. Change 792 L. 19 s. 7 d. of North Carolina into Pennsylvania currency. Facit 743 L. 8 s. $4\frac{1}{4}$ d.+

10. What sum of Maryland currency is equal to 6307 L. 13 s. 5 d. of New York? Ans. 5913 L. 8 s. $9\frac{3}{4}$ d.+

11. What is the value of a bill of 750 L., Pennsylvania currency, in New York or North Carolina currency? Ans. 800 L.

12. A merchant in Virginia consigns to his agent in New York a quantity of tobacco; which, when sold, and the charges deducted, amounts to 625 L. 6 s., what is the value thereof in Virginia currency; also in Federal Money?

Ans. { 468 L. 19 s. 6 d., Virginia currency.
1563 dols. 25 cts.

FOREIGN EXCHANGE.

Accounts are kept in England, Ireland, and the English West India Islands, in pounds, shillings, pence, and farthings; though their intrinsic values in these places are different.

A TABLE OF DIFFERENT MONEYS.

France.

12 Deniers - - -	1 Sol,
20 Sols - - - - -	1 Livre,
3 Livres - - -	1 Crown.

Spain.

4	Marvadies Vellon, or	1 Quarta,
$2\frac{1}{8}$	Marvadies of plate	
$8\frac{1}{2}$	Quartas, or	1 Rial Vellon,
34	Marvadies Vellon	
16	Quartas, or	1 Rial of plate,
34	Marvadies of plate	
8	Rials of plate - -	1 Piastre,
10	Rials of plate - -	1 Dollar,
5	Piastres - - -	1 Spanish Pistole.

Italy.

12	Deniers - - -	1 Sol,
20	Sols - - - - - -	1 Livre,
5	Livres - - - -	1 Piece of Eight at Genoa.
6	Livres - - - -	1 do at Leghorn,
6	Solidi - - - -	1 Gross,
24	Grosses -	1 Ducat.

Portugal.

400	Reas - - - -	1 Crusadoe,
1000	Reas - -	1 Millrea.

Holland.

8	Pennings - - -	1 Groat,
2	Groats - - -	1 Stiver, =2d.
6	Stivers - - -	1 Shilling,
20	Stivers - - -	1 Florin or Guilder,
$2\frac{1}{2}$	Florins - - -	1 Rix Dollar,
6	Florins - - -	1 £. Flemish.
5	Guilders* - - -	1 Ducat.

Denmark.

16	Shillings - - -	1 Mark,
6	Marks - - -	1 Rix Dollar,
32	Rustics - - -	1 Copper Dollar,
6	Copper Dollars -	1 Rix dollar.

* A stiver is estimated at 2 cents; and a florin or guilder at 40 cents, nearly.

Russia.

18	Pennings	- - - -	1 Gros,
30	Gros	- - - -	1 Florin,
3	Florins	- - -	1 Rix Dollar,
2	Rix Dollars	- - -	1 Gold Ducat.

All the operations in Exchange may be performed by the Rule of Three or by Practice.

Note.—The par of exchange between the United States and most other trading countries, may be ascertained by the table at page 63.

EXAMPLES.

1. A of Philadelphia is indebted to B of London 1474 L. 16 s. currency; how much sterling must be remitted, when the exchange is at 64 per cent.?

Ans. 899 L. 5 s. $4\frac{1}{4}$ d.

	L.	L. s.		L.	L. s. d.
As	164 :	1474 16	: :	100 :	899 5 $4\frac{1}{4}$

2. B of London is indebted to C of Philadelphia 943 L. 17 s. $5\frac{1}{4}$ d. sterling; for how much currency may C draw on B, exchange being at 64 per cent.?

L.		L.	s.	d.
50	$\frac{1}{2}$	943	17	$5\frac{1}{4}$
10	$\frac{1}{5}$	471	18	$8\frac{1}{2}$
2	$\frac{1}{5}$	94	7	$8\frac{3}{4}$
2	$\frac{1}{5}$	18	7	$6\frac{1}{2}$
		18	7	$6\frac{1}{2}$

Answer L. 1547 18 $11\frac{1}{2}$ currency.

3. C of Philadelphia is indebted to D of London 750 L. 2 s. $4\frac{1}{2}$ d. sterling; how much Pennsylvania currency will discharge the debt, exchange being at 78 per cent.? Ans. 1335 L. 4 s. $2\frac{1}{4}$ d.

4. How much sterling is equal to 1341 L. 9 s. $4\frac{3}{4}$ d., Pennsylvania currency, exchange being at $67\frac{1}{2}$ per cent.? Ans. 800 L. 17 s. $6\frac{1}{2}$ d.

5. Philadelphia. ———

Exchange for 452 L. 10 s. 6 d.

Thirty days after sight of this my first of exchange, second and third of like tenor and date not paid, pay to Samuel Sims, or order, four hundred and fifty-two pounds, ten shillings, and sixpence sterling, value received, which place to account of Peter Simpson.

To Samuel Jones, merchant,

London.

What is the value of this bill in Pennsylvania currency, exchange at $77\frac{1}{2}$ per cent.? Ans. 803 L. 4 s. $7\frac{1}{2}$ d.

6. M of Philadelphia owes P of London 1474 dollars 80 cents; how much sterling must be remitted when exchange is at par?

cts. *dols. cts.* *s. d.* *L. s. d.*

As 100 : 1474.80 :: 4 6 : 331 16 7. Ans.

7. What sum sterling is equal to 260 L. 8 s. 6 d. Virginia currency; exchange 44 per cent?

Ans. 180 L. 17 s.

8. M of Dublin draws upon M of London for 740 L. 14 s. 6 d. Irish; exchange at 12 per cent.: how much sterling will discharge this bill? Ans. 661 L. 7 s. $2\frac{3}{4}$ d.

9. P of London remits to G of Ireland 651 L. 14 s. $11\frac{3}{4}$ d. sterling; with how much Irish must P be credited, exchange being at 12 per cent.?

Ans. 729 L. 19 s. 2 d.

10. Purchased in Ireland goods to the value of 400 L. 17 s. 9 d. Irish; what sum Pennsylvania currency will discharge the debt, exchange being at $51\frac{1}{2}$ per cent.?

Ans. 607 L. 6 s. $10\frac{1}{2}$ d.

11. B of Jamaica is indebted to C of London 1470 L. 12 s. 8 d. sterling; with how much currency will C be credited at Jamaica, when exchange is at $36\frac{1}{2}$ per cent.?

Ans. 2007 L. 8 s. $3\frac{1}{4}$ d.

12. D of Jamaica is indebted to E of London 806 L. 5 s. sterling; with how much currency must E be credited in Jamaica, when the exchange is at 35 per cent.?

Ans. 1088 L. 8 s. 9 d.

13. P of Philadelphia received of A of Amsterdam, an invoice of goods amounting to 10235 florins, 17 stivers, 8 pennings; what sum of Pennsylvania currency will discharge the bill, at $35\frac{1}{4}$ d. per florin? and what is

the sum in sterling, exchange at 38 s. 6 d. Flemish per L. sterling? Ans. { 1503 L. 7 s. 10½ d. currency. 886 L. 4 s. 5½ d. sterling.

14. A merchant in Rotterdam has a bill drawn on him for 673 L. 16 s. 8 d. sterling, exchange at 33 s. 4 d. Flem. per pound sterling; how much Flemish must he pay? Ans. 1123 L. 1 s. 1¼ d.

15. A Connecticut merchant imported goods from France, amounting, per invoice, to 49008 livres; how much currency of that state, at 15 d. per livre, will they amount to? Ans. 3063 L. currency.

16. Philadelphia, ———

Exchange for 4226 livres, 12 sols, 8 deniers.

Thirty days after sight of this my second of exchange, (first of the same tenor and date not paid) pay to Thomas Broker, or order, four thousand two hundred and twenty-six livres, twelve sols, and eight deniers, value received; which place to account of

[illegible] Stroud.

To Thomas Lamot, Merchant,
Bordeaux.

How much sterling is the above bill, at 10½ d. per livre; and how much Pennsylvania currency, at 17½ d. per livre? Ans. { 184 L. 18 s. 3½ d. sterling. 308 L. 3 s. 10 d. currency.

17. What sum Pennsylvania currency is equal to 2524 piastres, 7 rials, 33 marv. at 7 s. 6 d. per piastre? Ans. 946 L. 17 s. 5½ d.

18. A merchant of North Carolina shipped a quantity of flour, which, when disposed of, amounted to 1186 millreas, 500 reas; and received in return 17 pipes of wine; how much was the wine per pipe, a millrea reckoned at 7 s. 6 d. Ans. 26 L. 3 s. 5¼ d.

19. A Virginia merchant sent goods to Norway, worth 1743 L. 16 s. Virginia currency; how many rix dollars, at 6 s. each, must he receive? Ans. 5812 dols. 4s.

Note.—To change bank into current money say: As 100 bank, is to 100 with the agio added; so is the bank given, to the current required.

To change current money into bank say: As 100 with the agio added, is to 100; so is the current given, to the bank required.

20. Change 794 guilders, 15 stivers, current money, into bank florins, agio $4\frac{5}{8}$ per cent.

Result 761 guild. 8 stiv. 11 pennings.

21. Change 761 guilders, 9 stivers bank, into current money, agio $4\frac{5}{8}$ per cent.

Result 794 guild. 15 stiv. 4 pennings.

22. A merchant in Holland wishes to change 4376 florins currency into bank, the agio at 4 per cent.; how many pounds Flemish bank must he receive?

Ans. 701 L. 1 flo. 13 stiv. 13 pen.

23. In 290 L. 11 s. 10 d., sterling, how many pounds Flemish; exchange at 33 s. 10 d. Flemish bank per pound sterling, and agio at $4\frac{1}{2}$ per cent.? Ans. 513 L. 14 s. 1 d.

24. A merchant in Philadelphia receives from London a parcel of goods, charged in the invoice at 450 L. 10 s. sterling, which he immediately sells at an advance of 78 per cent.; what is the amount in Pennsylvania currency; also in Federal money?

Ans. { 801 L. 17 s. $9\frac{1}{2}$d.
{ 2138 dols. $37\frac{1}{2}$ cts.

25. Amsterdam changes on London 34 s. 3 d. per L. sterling, and on Lisbon, at 52 d. Flemish for 400 reas; how then ought the exchange to go between London and Lisbon? Ans. $75\frac{3}{4}$ d.+sterling per millrea.

VULGAR FRACTIONS.

A vulgar fraction is a part, or parts of a unit or integer expressed by two numbers, placed one above the other, with a line drawn between them; as $\frac{1}{4}$ one fourth, $\frac{2}{3}$ two thirds.

The number above the line is called the *numerator*, and that below the line the *denominator*.

The denominator denotes the part, and the numerator informs how many of that part are designed to be expressed

Vulgar fractions are either proper, improper, compound, or mixed.

A *proper fraction* is that of which the numerator is less than the denominator; as $\frac{1}{2}$, $\frac{3}{4}$, $\frac{7}{8}$, &c.

An *improper fraction* is that of which the numerator is equal to, or greater than the denominator; as $\frac{4}{4}$, $\frac{7}{3}$, $\frac{12}{11}$, &c.

A *compound fraction* is a fraction of a fraction; as $\frac{1}{2}$ of $\frac{3}{4}$, or $\frac{2}{3}$ of $\frac{7}{8}$ of $\frac{9}{10}$, &c.

A *mixed number* consists of a whole number and a fraction; as $4\frac{3}{4}$, $7\frac{2}{3}$, &c.

REDUCTION OF VULGAR FRACTIONS.

CASE 1.

To reduce a fraction to its lowest terms.

RULE.

Divide the greater term by the less, and that divisor by the remainder, till nothing be left; the last divisor will be the common measure. Divide both terms by the common measure, and the quotients will be the numerator and denominator of the fraction required: or,

Divide the terms by any number that will divide them both without a remainder, and divide the quotients in the same manner, and so on, till no number greater than 1 will divide them; the fraction is then at its lowest terms.

Note.—If the common measure be 1, the fraction is already at its lowest terms. Cyphers on the right hand of both terms may be rejected; thus $\frac{400}{700}=\frac{4}{7}$.

EXAMPLES.

1. Reduce $\frac{72}{96}$ to its lowest terms.

```
            72)96)1                 Or thus:
               72              12)  2)
               —                  72/96 = 6/8 = 3/4 Result.
Com. measure 24)72(3
                72       24) 72/96 = 3/4 Result.
```

2. Reduce $\frac{9}{27}$ to its lowest terms. Result $\frac{1}{3}$.
3. Reduce $\frac{48}{56}$ to its lowest terms. Result $\frac{6}{7}$.
4. Reduce $\frac{72}{94}$ to its lowest terms. Result $\frac{36}{47}$.
5. Reduce $\frac{60}{125}$ to its lowest terms. Result $\frac{12}{25}$.
6. Reduce $\frac{84}{170}$ to its lowest terms. Result $\frac{42}{85}$.
7. Reduce $\frac{1344}{1536}$ to its lowest terms. Result $\frac{7}{8}$.

CASE 2.

To reduce several fractions to others of the same value, and having a common denominator.

RULE.

Multiply each numerator into all the denominators but its own, for its respective numerator; and all the denominators into each other, for a common denominator.

EXAMPLES.

1. Reduce $\frac{3}{4}$, $\frac{4}{5}$, and $\frac{5}{6}$ to a common denominator.

$$\left.\begin{matrix} 3\times5\times6=\ \ 90 \\ 4\times4\times6=\ \ 96 \\ 5\times4\times5=100 \end{matrix}\right\}\text{Numerators.}$$

$4\times5\times6=120$ Common denominator.

Result $\frac{90}{120}$, $\frac{96}{120}$, and $\frac{100}{120}$.

2. Reduce $\frac{1}{2}$, $\frac{3}{4}$, and $\frac{5}{8}$ to a common denominator.
Result $\frac{32}{64}$, $\frac{48}{64}$, $\frac{40}{64}$.
3. Reduce $\frac{1}{2}$, $\frac{2}{3}$, $\frac{5}{6}$, and $\frac{7}{8}$ to a common denominator.
Result $\frac{144}{288}$, $\frac{192}{288}$, $\frac{240}{288}$, $\frac{252}{288}$.
4. Reduce $\frac{7}{8}$, $\frac{2}{3}$, $\frac{3}{5}$, and $\frac{6}{7}$ to a common denominator.
Result $\frac{735}{840}$, $\frac{560}{840}$, $\frac{504}{840}$, $\frac{720}{840}$.
5. Reduce $\frac{4}{5}$, $\frac{1}{2}$, $\frac{5}{6}$, and $\frac{1}{4}$ to a common denominator.
Result $\frac{192}{240}$, $\frac{120}{240}$, $\frac{200}{240}$, $\frac{60}{240}$.

CASE 3.

To reduce a mixed number to an improper fraction.

RULE.

Multiply the whole number by the denominator of the fraction, and add the numerator to the product for a new numerator, under which place the given denominator.

EXAMPLES.

1. Reduce $12\frac{4}{9}$ to an improper fraction. Result $\frac{112}{9}$.

$12\times9+4=112$ new numerator. $\frac{112}{9}$ denominator.

2. Reduce $19\frac{12}{18}$ to an improper fraction. Result $\frac{354}{18}$.
3. Reduce $12\frac{4}{5}$ to an improper fraction. Result $\frac{64}{5}$.
4. Reduce $100\frac{19}{59}$ to an improper fraction.
Result $\frac{5919}{59}$.

5. Reduce $514\frac{5}{16}$ to an improper fraction.

Result $\frac{8229}{16}$.

6. Reduce $47\frac{3141}{8400}$ to an improper fraction.

Result $\frac{397941}{8400}$.

CASE 4.

To reduce an improper fraction to a whole or mixed number

RULE.

Divide the upper term by the lower.

Note.—This case and case 3 prove each other.

EXAMPLES.

1. Reduce $\frac{219}{17}$ to its proper terms. Result $12\frac{5}{17}$.

```
17)219(12 5/17
   17
   --
    49
    34
    --
    15
    --
    17
```

2. Reduce $\frac{317}{19}$ to its proper terms. Result $16\frac{13}{19}$.
3. Reduce $\frac{141}{17}$ to its proper terms. Result $8\frac{5}{17}$.
4. Reduce $\frac{126}{48}$ to its proper terms. Result $2\frac{5}{8}$.
5. Reduce $\frac{3848}{21}$ to its proper terms. Result $183\frac{5}{21}$.
6. Reduce $\frac{1245}{22}$ to its proper terms. Result $56\frac{13}{22}$.

CASE 5.

To reduce a compound fraction to a single one.

RULE.

Multiply the numerators together for a new numerator, and all the denominators for a new denominator.

Note.—Like figures in the numerators and denominators may be cancelled, and frequently others contracted, by taking their aliquot parts.

EXAMPLES.

1. Reduce $\frac{2}{3}$ of $\frac{3}{4}$ of $\frac{4}{5}$ to a single fraction. Result $\frac{2}{5}$.

$$\frac{2\times3\times4=24}{3\times4\times5=60}=\frac{2}{5}. \qquad \text{Or, } \frac{2}{3} \text{ of } \frac{3}{4} \text{ of } \frac{4}{5}=\frac{24}{60}=\frac{2}{5}.$$

Or cancelled, $\frac{2}{\cancel{3}}$ of $\frac{\cancel{3}}{\cancel{4}}$ of $\frac{\cancel{4}}{5}=\frac{2}{5}$ as before.

2. Reduce $\frac{3}{4}$ of $\frac{5}{6}$ of $\frac{9}{10}$ to a single fraction.
Result $\frac{135}{240}=\frac{9}{16}$.

3. Reduce $\frac{4}{5}$ of $\frac{5}{8}$ of $\frac{7}{9}$ to a single fraction.
Result $\frac{140}{360}=\frac{7}{18}$.

4. Reduce $\frac{2}{7}$ of $\frac{7}{8}$ of $\frac{8}{9}$ to a single fraction.
Result $\frac{112}{504}=\frac{2}{9}$.

5. Reduce $\frac{11}{12}$ of $\frac{13}{14}$ of $\frac{21}{29}$ to a single fraction.
Result $\frac{3003}{4872}=\frac{143}{232}$.

6. Reduce $\frac{12}{14}$ of $\frac{5}{6}$ of $\frac{1}{2}$ to a single fraction.
Result $\frac{60}{168}=\frac{5}{14}$.

CASE 6.

To reduce the fraction of one denomination to the fraction of another, but greater, retaining the same value.

RULE.

Make the fraction a compound one, by comparing it with all the denominations between it and that to which it is to be reduced; which fraction reduce to a single one.

EXAMPLES.

1. Reduce $\frac{5}{6}$ of a penny to the fraction of a pound.
$\frac{5}{6}$ of $\frac{1}{12}$ of $\frac{1}{20}=\frac{5}{1440}=\frac{1}{288}$ of a pound.

2. Reduce $\frac{4}{5}$ of a penny to the fraction of a pound.
Result $\frac{1}{300}$ L.

3. Reduce $\frac{1}{2}$ of a farthing to the fraction of a shilling.
Result $\frac{1}{96}$ s.

4. Reduce $\frac{5}{9}$ of a cent to the fraction of a dollar.
Result $\frac{1}{180}$ dol.

5. Reduce $\frac{8}{9}$ of an oz., troy, to the fraction of a pound.
Result $\frac{2}{27}$ lb.

6. Reduce $\frac{6}{7}$ of a lb. avoirdupois to the fraction of a cwt. Result $\frac{3}{392}$ cwt.

7. Reduce $\frac{9}{13}$ of a pint of wine to the fraction of a hhd. Result $\frac{1}{728}$ hhd.

8. Reduce $\frac{10}{11}$ of a minute to the fraction of a day. Result $\frac{1}{1584}$ day.

CASE 7.

To reduce the fraction of one denomination to the fraction of another, but less, retaining the same value.

RULE.

Multiply the given numerator by the parts of the denomination between it and that to which it is to be reduced, for a new numerator, and place it over the given denominator; which reduce to its lowest terms.

Note.—This case and case 6 prove each other.

EXAMPLES.

1. Reduce $\frac{5}{1440}$ of a pound to the fraction of a penny.

$5\times20\times12=\frac{1200}{1440}=\frac{5}{6}$ d. Result.

2. Reduce $\frac{4}{1200}$ of a pound to the fraction of a penny. Result $\frac{4}{5}$ d.

3. Reduce $\frac{1}{96}$ of a shilling to the fraction of a farthing. Result $\frac{1}{2}$ qr.

4. Reduce $\frac{1}{180}$ of a dollar to the fraction of a cent. Result $\frac{5}{9}$ ct.

5. Reduce $\frac{2}{27}$ of a lb. troy to the fraction of an oz. Result $\frac{8}{9}$ oz.

6. Reduce $\frac{3}{392}$ of a cwt. to the fraction of a lb. avoirdupois. Result $\frac{6}{7}$ lb.

7. Reduce $\frac{1}{728}$ of a hhd. to the fraction of a pint. Result $\frac{9}{13}$ pt.

8. Reduce $\frac{1}{1584}$ of a day to the fraction of a minute. Result $\frac{10}{11}$.

CASE 8.

To reduce a fraction to its proper value or quantity in integers.

RULE.

Multiply the numerator by the known parts of the integer, and divide by the denominator.

EXAMPLES.

1. Reduce $\frac{2}{3}$ of a pound to its proper value.

2 thirds of a pound.
20
—
3)40 thirds of a shilling.
—
13 s. + 1 third of a shilling
12
—
3)12 thirds of a penny.
—
4 d. Result 13 s. 4 d.

Or thus:
L. L.
$\frac{2}{3}$ of $\frac{20}{1} = \frac{40}{3} = 13$ s. 4 d.

2. Reduce $\frac{2}{6}$ of a pound to its proper value. Result 6 s. 8 d.

3. Reduce $\frac{18}{43}$ of a shilling to its proper value. Result 5 d. $\frac{1}{43}$.

4. Reduce $\frac{6}{7}$ of 5 L. 9 s. to its proper value. Result 4 L. 13 s. 5 d. $\frac{1}{7}$.

5. Reduce $\frac{3}{5}$ of a dollar to its proper value. Result 60 cents.

6. Reduce $\frac{12}{16}$ of a lb. troy to its proper quantity. Result 9 oz.

7. Reduce $\frac{5}{9}$ of a lb. avoirdupois to its proper quantity. Result 8 oz. 14 dr. $\frac{2}{9}$.

8. Reduce $\frac{12}{78}$ of a ton to its proper quantity. Result 3 cwt. 8 lb. 9 oz. 13 dr. $\frac{42}{78}$.

9. Reduce $\frac{4}{7}$ of a mile to its proper quantity. Result 4 fur. 125 yds. 2 ft. 1 in. $\frac{5}{7}$.

10. Reduce $\frac{9}{10}$ of a yard to its proper quantity. Result 2 ft. 8 in. $\frac{2}{5}$.

11. Reduce $\frac{7}{16}$ of an acre to its proper quantity. Result 1 rood 30 perches.

12. Reduce $\frac{4}{9}$ of a ton of wine to its proper quantity. Result 1 hhd. 49 gal.

13. Reduce $\frac{7}{8}$ of a yard of cloth to its proper quantity. Result 3 qrs. 2 nails.

14. Reduce $\frac{9}{10}$ of a year to its proper quantity. Result 328 days 12 hours.

CASE 9.

To reduce any given value, or quantity, to a fraction of any greater denomination of the same kind.

RULE.

Reduce the given quantity to the lowest denomination mentioned for a numerator, and the integer into the same denomination for a denominator.

Note.—If a fraction be given, multiply both parts by the denominator thereof, and to the numerator add the numerator of the given fraction.

EXAMPLES.

1. Reduce 13 s. 4 d. to the fraction of a pound.

$$\frac{13 \text{ s. } 4 \text{ d.} = 160 \text{ d.}}{1 \text{ L.} = 20 \text{ s.} = 240 \text{ d.}} = \tfrac{2}{3} \text{ L.}$$

2. Reduce 10 s. 6 d. to the fraction of a pound. Result $\frac{21}{40}$ L.

3. Reduce $4\frac{1}{2}$ d. to the fraction of a shilling. Result $\frac{3}{8}$ s.

4. Reduce $5\frac{1}{43}$ d. to the fraction of a shilling. Result $\frac{18}{43}$ s.

5. Reduce 9 oz. troy to the fraction of a lb. Result $\frac{3}{4}$ lb.

6. Reduce 9 oz. 2 dr. $\frac{2}{7}$ avoirdupois to the fraction of a pound. Result $\frac{4}{7}$.

7. Reduce 3 cwt. 8 lb. 9 oz. 13 dr. $\frac{7}{13}$, to the fraction of a ton. Result $\frac{2}{13}$ ton.

8. Reduce 3 qr. 2 na. to the fraction of a yard. Result $\frac{7}{8}$ yd.

9. Reduce 6 furlongs 16 poles to the fraction of a mile. Result $\frac{4}{5}$.

10. Reduce 2 roods 20 perches to the fraction of an acre. Result $\frac{5}{8}$.

ADDITION OF VULGAR FRACTIONS.

GENERAL RULE.

Reduce the given fractions, if necessary, to single ones, and to a common denominator; then add all the numerators together, and place the sum over the common denominator.

If fractions be of different denominations, find their value separately, and add as in Compound Addition.

EXAMPLES.

Note 1.—*When the given fractions have a common denominator, add their numerators together, and place the sum over the common denominator.*

1. Add $\frac{1}{7}$, $\frac{2}{7}$, and $\frac{3}{7}$ together. Result $\frac{6}{7}$.

$$\frac{1}{7}+\frac{2}{7}+\frac{3}{7}=\frac{6}{7}\ \begin{matrix}\text{sum of the numerators.}\\ \text{common denominator.}\end{matrix}$$

2. Add $\frac{2}{9}$, $\frac{3}{9}$, and $\frac{1}{9}$ together. Result $\frac{6}{9}$.
3. Add $\frac{3}{17}$, $\frac{5}{17}$, and $\frac{7}{17}$ together. Result $\frac{15}{17}$.
4. Add $\frac{2}{15}$, $\frac{5}{15}$, and $\frac{8}{15}$ together. Result 1.
5. Add $\frac{1}{9}$, $\frac{2}{9}$, $\frac{4}{9}$, $\frac{5}{9}$, and $\frac{7}{9}$ together. Result $2\frac{1}{9}$.

Note 2.—*When the given fractions have not a common denominator, reduce them to such as have, by Rule in Case* 2 *of Reduction; then add, as in the foregoing examples.*

6. Add $\frac{1}{4}$ and $\frac{3}{5}$ together. Result $\frac{17}{20}$.

$$\left.\begin{matrix}1\times5=\ 5\\ 3\times4=12\end{matrix}\right\}\text{numerators.}\qquad \frac{17}{4\times5=20}\ \text{com. denom.}$$

$$17\ \text{sum.}$$

7. Add $\frac{1}{8}$, $\frac{3}{10}$, and $\frac{4}{12}$ together. Result $\frac{728}{960}=\frac{91}{120}$.
8. Add $\frac{2}{3}$ and $\frac{5}{7}$ together. Result $1\frac{8}{21}$.
9. Add $\frac{7}{10}$, $\frac{11}{12}$, and $\frac{4}{9}$ together. Result $2\frac{11}{180}$.

Note 3.—*When mixed numbers are given, add the fractions as under note* 1 or 2; *then, if their sum be an improper fraction, reduce it to a mixed number, and add its integers to the given integers; but if it be not an improper fraction, annex it to the sum of the given integers.*

10. Add $5\frac{2}{3}$, $6\frac{7}{8}$, and $4\frac{1}{2}$ together. Result $17\frac{1}{24}$.

Fractions

$$\frac{2}{3}+\frac{7}{8}+\frac{1}{2}=2\frac{1}{24}$$

$$\text{Integers}\left\{\begin{matrix}5\\6\\4\end{matrix}\right.$$

Sum of fractions $2\frac{1}{24}$.

$17\frac{1}{24}$.

11. Add $2\frac{1}{2}$ and $3\frac{3}{4}$ together. Result $6\frac{1}{4}$.
12. Add $7\frac{3}{7}$ and $5\frac{4}{9}$ together. Result $12\frac{55}{63}$.
13. Add $17\frac{1}{2}$ and $\frac{2}{3}$ together. Result $18\frac{1}{6}$.
14. Add 4, 6, 9, $\frac{3}{4}$, and $\frac{5}{9}$ together. Result $20\frac{11}{36}$.
15. Add 5, $7\frac{1}{2}$, $\frac{2}{5}$, and $\frac{7}{11}$ together. Result $13\frac{59}{110}$.

Note 4.—*When compound fractions are given, reduce them to single fractions, and proceed as before.*

16. Add $\frac{5}{6}$ of $\frac{9}{10}$, and $\frac{7}{12}$ of $\frac{4}{5}$ together. Result $1\frac{13}{60}$.

$$\frac{5}{6} \text{ of } \frac{9}{10} = \frac{45}{60} \qquad \frac{28}{60} + \frac{45}{60} = 1\frac{13}{60}.$$
$$\frac{7}{12} \text{ of } \frac{4}{5} = \frac{28}{60}$$

17. Add $\frac{2}{4}$ of $\frac{7}{8}$ and $\frac{4}{6}$ of $\frac{10}{20}$ together. Result $\frac{37}{48}$.
18. Add $1\frac{3}{5}$, $\frac{4}{5}$ of $\frac{1}{3}$, and $9\frac{3}{20}$ together. Result $11\frac{1}{60}$.
19. Add $1\frac{9}{10}$, $6\frac{7}{8}$, $\frac{2}{3}$ of $\frac{1}{2}$, and $7\frac{1}{2}$ together. Result $16\frac{73}{120}$.

Note 5.—*When the given fractions are of several denominations, reduce them to their proper values or quantities, and add as in the following example:*

20. Add $\frac{7}{9}$ of a pound to $\frac{3}{10}$ of a shilling. Result 15 s. $10\frac{4}{15}$ d.

	s.	*d.*		*s.*	*d.*
$\frac{7}{9}$ of a *L.* =	15	$6\frac{2}{3}$	*d.* *d.* *d.*	15	6
$\frac{3}{10}$ of a *s.* =	0	$3\frac{3}{5}$	$\frac{2}{3} + \frac{3}{5} = 1\frac{4}{15}$	0	3
					$1\frac{4}{15}$
				15	$10\frac{4}{15}$

21. Add $\frac{7}{8}$ of a pound to $\frac{3}{4}$ of a shilling. Result 18 s. 3 d.
22. Add $\frac{3}{4}$ of a penny to $\frac{1}{9}$ of a pound. Result 2 s. 3 d. 1 qr. $\frac{2}{3}$.
23. Add $\frac{1}{2}$ lb. troy to $\frac{7}{12}$ of an ounce. Result 6 oz. 11 dwt. 16 grs.
24. Add $\frac{3}{4}$ of a mile to $\frac{7}{10}$ of a furlong. Result 6 furlongs 28 poles.
25. Add $\frac{1}{2}$ of a yard to $\frac{2}{3}$ of a foot. Result 2 ft. 2 in.
26. Add $\frac{1}{3}$ of a day to $\frac{1}{2}$ of an hour. Result 8 h. 30 min.
27. Add $\frac{1}{3}$ of a week, $\frac{1}{4}$ of a day, and $\frac{1}{2}$ of an hour together. Result 2 days, 14 hours, 30 min.

SUBTRACTION OF VULGAR FRACTIONS.

GENERAL RULE.

Prepare the given fractions as in Addition, then subtract the less numerator from the greater, and place the difference over the common denominator.

EXAMPLES.

1. From $\frac{4}{5}$ take $\frac{3}{5}$. Result $\frac{1}{5}$.
2. From $\frac{7}{12}$ take $\frac{4}{12}$. Result $\frac{1}{4}$.
3. From $\frac{9}{10}$ take $\frac{5}{10}$. Result $\frac{2}{5}$.

Note 1.—*When the given fractions have not a common denominator, reduce them to such as have, and then subtract as before.*

4. From $\frac{3}{7}$ take $\frac{2}{5}$. Result $\frac{1}{35}$.

$$\left.\begin{array}{l} 3 \times 5 = 15 \\ 2 \times 7 = 14 \end{array}\right\} \text{new numerators.}$$

$$5 \times 7 = 35 \text{ com. denom.}$$

$$\frac{1}{35}$$

5. From $\frac{7}{12}$ take $\frac{1}{4}$. Result $\frac{1}{3}$.
6. From $\frac{11}{12}$ take $\frac{2}{3}$. Result $\frac{1}{4}$.
7. From $\frac{5}{8}$ take $\frac{1}{2}$. Result $\frac{1}{8}$.
8. From $\frac{7}{15}$ take $\frac{9}{20}$. Result $\frac{1}{60}$.

Note 2.—*When mixed numbers are given, reduce them to improper fractions, and reduce these improper fractions to such as have a common denominator; then subtract as before.*

9. From $8\frac{2}{9}$ take $6\frac{3}{11}$. Result $1\frac{94}{99}$.
10. From $9\frac{1}{5}$ take $4\frac{3}{4}$. Result $4\frac{9}{20}$.
11. From $7\frac{7}{8}$ take $3\frac{2}{3}$. Result $4\frac{5}{24}$.

Note 3.—*When compound fractions are given, reduce them to single ones, and reduce these single fractions to such as have a common denominator; then subtract as before.*

12. From $\frac{1}{2}$ of $\frac{9}{10}$ take $\frac{1}{4}$ of $\frac{4}{9}$. Result $\frac{61}{180}$.
13. From $\frac{3}{4}$ of $\frac{11}{12}$ take $\frac{1}{5}$ of $\frac{2}{3}$. Result $\frac{133}{240}$.
14. From $\frac{5}{6}$ take $\frac{3}{5}$ of $\frac{5}{8}$. Result $\frac{11}{24}$.

Note 4.—*When a fraction or a mixed number is to be subtracted from a whole number, subtract the numerator of the fraction from its denominator, and under the remainder set the denominator; then carry it to be subtracted from the integers.*

15. From 6 take $\frac{1}{8}$. Result $5\frac{7}{8}$.
16. From 3 take $\frac{3}{16}$. Result $2\frac{13}{16}$.
17. From 100 take $99\frac{99}{100}$. Result $\frac{1}{100}$.

Note 5.—*When the given fractions are of different denominations, reduce them to their proper values, or quantities, and subtract as in the following example.*

18. From $\frac{7}{9}$ of a pound, take $\frac{3}{10}$ of a shilling.

$\frac{7}{9}$ of a L. = 15 s. $6\frac{2}{3}$ d.   *d.* *d.*
$\frac{3}{10}$ of a s. = $3\frac{3}{5}$ d. $\frac{2}{3} - \frac{3}{5} = \frac{1}{15}$.

15 s. $3\frac{1}{15}$ d. Result.

19. From $\frac{3}{4}$ of a L. take $\frac{3}{4}$ of a shilling.
Result 14 s. 3 d.
20. From $\frac{3}{4}$ of a lb. troy, take $\frac{1}{6}$ of an ounce.
Result 8 oz. 16 dwt. 16 grs.
21. From $\frac{1}{6}$ of a yard take $\frac{2}{3}$ of an inch.
Result 5 in. $\frac{1}{3}$.
22. From $\frac{5}{9}$ of a L. take $\frac{2}{3}$ of $\frac{3}{4}$ of a shilling.
Result 10 s. 7 d. 1 qr. $\frac{1}{3}$.

MULTIPLICATION OF VULGAR FRACTIONS.

GENERAL RULE.

Reduce compound fractions to single ones, and mixed numbers to improper fractions; then multiply the numerators together for a new numerator, and the denominators for a new denominator.

EXAMPLES.

1. Multiply $\frac{4}{9}$ by $\frac{2}{7}$. Result $\frac{8}{63}$.
2. Multiply $\frac{1}{12}$ by $\frac{3}{8}$. Result $\frac{1}{32}$.
3. Multiply $\frac{6}{7}$ by $\frac{18}{6}$. Result $2\frac{24}{42}$.

4. Multiply $12\frac{3}{5}$ by $7\frac{2}{3}$. Result $96\frac{3}{5}$.
$12\frac{3}{5}=\frac{63}{5}$ and $7\frac{2}{3}=\frac{23}{3}$; then $\frac{63}{5}\times\frac{23}{3}=\frac{1449}{15}=96\frac{3}{5}$.
5 Multiply $7\frac{1}{4}$ by $8\frac{1}{2}$. Result $61\frac{5}{8}$.
6. Multiply $4\frac{1}{2}$ by $\frac{1}{8}$. Result $\frac{9}{16}$.
7. Multiply $\frac{7}{8}$ by $13\frac{9}{10}$. Result $12\frac{13}{80}$.
8. Multiply $\frac{1}{3}$ of $\frac{4}{5}$ by $\frac{7}{10}$ of $\frac{11}{12}$. Result $\frac{77}{450}$.
9. Multiply $4\frac{3}{4}$ by $\frac{2}{3}$ of $\frac{3}{4}$. Result $2\frac{3}{8}$.
10. Multiply $\frac{1}{2}$ of 7 by $\frac{3}{6}$. Result $1\frac{3}{4}$.
11. Multiply $2\frac{1}{3}$ by $1\frac{1}{7}$, and multiply the product by $\frac{1}{2}$ of $\frac{3}{4}$ of $\frac{2}{3}$. Result $\frac{2}{3}$.

DIVISION OF VULGAR FRACTIONS.

GENERAL RULE.

Prepare the given fractions, if necessary, then invert the divisor, and proceed as in Multiplication.

EXAMPLES.

1. Divide $\frac{4}{9}$ by $\frac{7}{8}$. Result $\frac{32}{63}$.

$$\frac{8\times4=32}{7\times9=63}$$

2. Divide $\frac{4}{7}$ by $\frac{2}{3}$. Result $\frac{6}{7}$.
3. Divide $\frac{17}{21}$ by $\frac{3}{5}$. Result $1\frac{22}{63}$.
4. Divide $1\frac{1}{2}$ by $4\frac{8}{10}$. Result $\frac{5}{16}$.
5. Divide $3\frac{1}{6}$ by $9\frac{1}{2}$. Result $\frac{1}{3}$.
6. Divide $\frac{7}{8}$ by 4. Result $\frac{7}{32}$.
7. Divide 4 by $\frac{7}{8}$. Result $4\frac{4}{7}$.
8. Divide $\frac{1}{2}$ of $\frac{2}{3}$ by $\frac{2}{3}$ of $\frac{3}{4}$. Result $\frac{2}{3}$.
9. Divide $\frac{1}{5}$ of 19 by $\frac{2}{3}$ of $\frac{3}{4}$. Result $7\frac{3}{5}$.
10. Divide $4\frac{5}{9}$ by $\frac{5}{9}$ of 4. Result $2\frac{1}{20}$.
11. Divide $\frac{2}{3}$ of $\frac{1}{3}$ by $\frac{5}{7}$ of $7\frac{3}{5}$. Result $\frac{7}{171}$.
12. Divide $5205\frac{1}{5}$ by $\frac{4}{5}$ of 91. Result $71\frac{1}{2}$.

THE SINGLE RULE OF THREE,

IN VULGAR FRACTIONS.

RULE.

Prepare the given terms, if necessary, and state them as in whole numbers; multiply the second and third terms together, and divide the product by the first. Or,

Invert the dividing term, and multiply the three terms together, as in Multiplication.

EXAMPLES.

1. If $\frac{1}{4}$ of a yard cost $\frac{2}{3}$ of a shilling, what will $\frac{7}{8}$ of a yard come to? Ans. 2 s. 4 d.

yd. *yd.* *s.* *s.*

If $\frac{1}{4} : \frac{7}{8} : \frac{2}{3} : \frac{56}{24}$ s. $=2$ s. 4 d.

Inverted $\frac{4}{1}\times\frac{7}{8}\times\frac{2}{3}=\frac{56}{24}=2$ s. 4 d.

2. If $\frac{3}{5}$ of a yard cost $\frac{7}{15}$ of a pound, what will $\frac{3}{14}$ of a yard come to? Ans. 3 s. 4 d.

3. If $\frac{11}{13}$ of a lb. of sugar cost $\frac{7}{15}$ of a shilling, what cost $\frac{32}{43}$ of a lb.? Ans. 4 d. 3 qrs. $\frac{1057}{2365}$.

4. If $\frac{3}{4}$ of a yard of lawn cost 7 s 3 d. what will $10\frac{1}{3}$ yards cost? Ans. 4 L. 19 s. 10 d. 2 qrs. $\frac{2}{3}$.

5. If $1\frac{1}{4}$ yard cost 9 s., what is the value of $16\frac{1}{4}$ yards? Ans. 5 L. 17 s.

6. What is the value of 100 yards of cloth, at $1\frac{1}{5}$ shillings per yard? Ans. 6 L.

7. If 1 ounce of silver cost $5\frac{1}{2}$ s., what is the value of $16\frac{11}{15}$ oz.? Ans. 4 L. 12 s. $1\frac{3}{5}$ qrs.

8. How much will $4\frac{5}{9}$ lb. of cheese come to, at $12\frac{1}{5}$ cents per lb.? Ans. $55\frac{26}{45}$ cents.

9. What will $\frac{8}{9}$ of a pound come to, if $\frac{7}{8}$ of a lb. cost $\frac{2}{5}$ of a shilling? Ans. $4\frac{92}{105}$ d.

10. If one yard of cloth cost $15\frac{5}{8}$ s., what will 4 pieces, each containing $27\frac{3}{8}$ yards, cost? Ans. 85 L. 10 s. $11\frac{1}{4}$ d.

11. A person having $\frac{4}{5}$ of a sloop, sells $\frac{2}{3}$ of his share for 319 L., what is the value of the whole vessel at that rate? Ans. 598 L. 2 s. 6 d.

12. A merchant had $5\frac{8}{9}$ cwt. of sugar, at $6\frac{3}{4}$ d. per lb., which he bartered for tea, at $8\frac{5}{8}$ s. per lb. How much tea did he receive for the sugar? Ans. $43\frac{1}{69}$ lb.

INVERSE PROPORTION.

1. How much shalloon, $\frac{3}{4}$ of a yard wide, will line $4\frac{1}{2}$ yards of cloth, $1\frac{1}{2}$ yard wide? Ans. 9 yards.

$4\frac{1}{2}=\frac{9}{2}$ *yd. yd. yd. yd.*   Or thus:

$1\frac{1}{2}=\frac{3}{2}$ As $\frac{3}{2} : \frac{3}{4} :: \frac{9}{2} : 9$ $\frac{3}{2}\times\frac{4}{3}\times\frac{9}{2}=\frac{108}{12}=9.$

2. What quantity of shalloon, $\frac{3}{4}$ yard wide, will line $7\frac{1}{2}$ yards of cloth, $1\frac{1}{2}$ yards wide? Ans. 15 yards.

3. If 16 men finish a piece of work in $28\frac{1}{5}$ days, how long will 12 men require to do the same work? Ans. $37\frac{3}{5}$ days.

4. If 3 men can do a piece of work in $4\frac{1}{2}$ hours, in how many hours will 10 men do the same? Ans. $1\frac{7}{20}$.

5. How many pieces of cloth, at $20\frac{1}{8}$ dollars per piece, are equal in value to $240\frac{1}{7}$ pieces, at $12\frac{1}{2}$ dollars per piece? Ans. $149\frac{177}{1127}$ pieces.

6. A merchant bartered $5\frac{8}{9}$ cwt. of sugar, at $6\frac{3}{4}$ d. per lb., for tea, at $8\frac{5}{8}$ s. per lb. How much tea did he receive? Ans. $43\frac{1}{69}$ lb.

THE DOUBLE RULE OF THREE,

IN VULGAR FRACTIONS.

RULE.

Prepare the given terms, when necessary, by reduction, then proceed as directed in whole numbers. Or,

Invert the dividing terms, and multiply the upper figures continually for the numerator, and those below for the denominator of the fractional answer.

EXAMPLES.

1. If $\frac{3}{4}$ yard of cloth, $\frac{7}{8}$ yard wide, cost $\frac{2}{5}$ L., what is the value of $\frac{5}{8}$ yard, $1\frac{3}{4}$ yards wide, of the same quality?

$$\left.\begin{array}{l}\frac{3}{4}\text{ yd.} : \frac{5}{8}\text{ yd.}\\ \frac{7}{8}\text{ yd.} : \frac{7}{4}\text{ yd.}\end{array}\right\} :: \frac{2}{5}\text{ L.} : \left\{\begin{array}{l}\frac{3}{4}\times\frac{7}{8}=\frac{21}{32}\\ \frac{5}{8}\times\frac{7}{4}\times\frac{2}{5}=\frac{70}{160}=\frac{7}{16}.\end{array}\right.$$

$$\frac{7}{16}\div\frac{21}{32}=\frac{224}{336}=\frac{2}{3}\text{ L.}=13\text{ s. }4\text{ d. Answer.}$$

2. If $2\frac{1}{4}$ yards of cloth, $1\frac{3}{5}$ yd. wide, cost $3\frac{3}{5}$ L., what is the value of $38\frac{1}{4}$ yds. 2 yds. wide?

Ans. 76 L. 10 s.

3. If 3 men receive $8\frac{9}{10}$ L. for $19\frac{1}{2}$ days' labor, how much must 20 men have for $100\frac{1}{4}$ days?

Ans. 305 L. 0 s. $8\frac{8}{39}$ d.

4. If 50 L. in 5 months gain $2\frac{37}{144}$ L. interest, in what time will $13\frac{1}{8}$ L. gain $1\frac{1}{12}$ L.?

Ans. in 9 months.

5. If the carriage of 60 cwt. 20 miles cost $14\frac{1}{2}$ dollars, what weight can I have carried 30 miles for $5\frac{7}{16}$ dollars?

Ans. 15 cwt.

DECIMAL FRACTIONS.

A Decimal Fraction is a fraction whose denominator is 1, with as many cyphers annexed as there are places in the numerator, and is usually expressed by writing the numerator only with a point prefixed to it: thus $\frac{5}{10}$, $\frac{75}{100}$, $\frac{625}{1000}$, are decimal fractions, and are expressed by .5, .75, .625.

A mixed number, consisting of a whole number and a decimal, as $25\frac{5}{10}$, is written thus, 25.5.

As in numeration of whole numbers the values of the figures increase in a tenfold proportion, from the right hand to the left; so in decimals, their values decrease in the same proportion, from the left hand to the right, which is exemplified in the following

TABLE.

Hundred million.	Ten million.	Million.	Hundred thousand.	Ten thousand.	Thousand.	Hundred.	Ten.	Unit.		Tenth.	Hundredth.	Thousandth.	Ten thousandth.	Hundred thousandth.	Millionth.	Ten millionth.	Hundred millionth.	Thousand millionth.
1	1	1	1	1	1	1	1	1	.	1	1	1	1	1	1	1	1	1

Whole numbers. Decimals.

Note.—Ciphers annexed to decimals, neither increase nor decrease their value; thus, .5, .50, .500, being $\frac{5}{10}$, $\frac{50}{100}$, $\frac{500}{1000}$, are of the same value: but ciphers prefixed to decimals, decrease them in a tenfold proportion; thus .5, .05, .005; being $\frac{5}{10}$, $\frac{5}{100}$, $\frac{5}{1000}$, are of different values.

ADDITION OF DECIMALS.

RULE.

Place the given numbers according to their values, viz., units under units, tenths under tenths, &c., and add as in addition of whole numbers; observing to set the point in the sum exactly under those of the given numbers.

EXAMPLES.

.12	2.16	.14	.1	.15
.134	3.45	.24	4.12	.75
.21	40.02	.122	15.4	.92
.743	35.4	.36	76.36	63.25
.345	36.1	.141	120.16	25.
.002	125.32	.567	425.04	4.
1.554	242.45			

6 Add .5, .75, .125, .496, and .750 together.

7. Add .15, 126.5, 650.17, 940.113, and 722.2560 together.

8. Add 420., 372.45, .270, 965.02, and 1.1756 together.

SUBTRACTION OF DECIMALS.

RULE.

Place the numbers as in addition, with the less under the greater, and subtract as in whole numbers; setting the point in the remainder under those in the given numbers.

EXAMPLES.

.4562	56.12	4314	5672.1	32.456
.316	1.242	.312	321.12	1.33
.1402	54.878			

6. From 100.17 take 1.146.
7. From 146.265 take 45.3278.
8. From 4560. take .720.

MULTIPLICATION OF DECIMALS.

RULE.

Multiply as in whole numbers: then observe how many decimal figures there are in both factors, and point off that many figures, for decimals, in the product.

If there are not so many figures in the product as there are decimal figures in both factors, prefix ciphers to supply the deficiency.

EXAMPLES.

1. Multiply .612 by 4.12

```
   .612
   4.12
  -----
   1224
   612
 2448
-------
2.52144
```

2. Multiply 1.007 by .041

```
  1.007
   .041
 ------
   1007
  4028
 ------
.041287
```

3. Multiply	37.9 by 46.5	Product	1762.35
4. ———	36.5 by 7.27	——	265.355
5. ———	29.831 by .952	——	28.399112
6. ———	3.92 by 196.	——	768.32
7. ———	.285 by .003	——	.000855
8. ———	4.001 by .004	——	.016004
9. ———	.00071 by .121	——	.00008591

Note.—Multiplication of decimals may be contracted thus:

Write the units place of the multiplier under that figure of the multiplicand whose place you would reserve in the product; and dispose of the rest of the figures in a contrary order to what they are usually placed in. In multiplying, reject all the figures that are to the right hand of the multiplying digit, and set down the products, so that their right hand figures may fall in a straight line below each other; observing to increase the first figure of every line with what would arise by carrying 1 from 5 to 15, 2 from 15 to 25, &c., from the preceding figures when you begin to multiply, and the sum is the product required.

EXAMPLES.

1. Multiply 27.14986 by 92.41035, so as to retain only four decimal places in the product.

Contracted.	Common way.
27.14986	27.14986
53014.29	92.41035
24434874	13574930
542997	8144958
108599	2714986
2715	10859944
81	5429972
14	24434874
2508.9280	2508.9280650510

2. Multiply 245.378263 by 72.4385, reserving 5 decimal places in the product. Prod. 17774.83330.

3. Multiply .243264 by .725234, reserving 6 decimal places in the product. Prod. .180049.

DIVISION OF DECIMALS.

RULE.

Divide as in whole numbers; then observe how many more decimal figures there are in the dividend than in the divisor, and point off that many figures, for decimals, in the quotient.

If there are not so many figures in the quotient as the

rule directs to be pointed off, prefix cyphers to supply the defect.

If, after dividing, there be a remainder, cyphers may be affixed to the dividend, as decimal figures, and the quotient carried on to greater exactness.

If there are more decimal figures in the divisor than there are in the dividend, the number of decimal figures in the dividend must be increased by affixing cyphers.

EXAMPLES.

1. Divide .863972 by .92

```
.92).863972(.9391
     828
     ---
      359
      276
      ---
       837
       828
       ---
         92
         92
         --
```

2. Divide 4.13 by 572.4

```
572.4)4.130000(.00721+
      40068
      -----
       12320
       11448
       -----
         8720
         5724
         ----
         2996
```

3.	Divide 19.25 by 38.5	Quotient	.5
4.	——— 234.70525 by 64.25	———	3.653
5.	——— 1.0012 by .075	———	13.34+
6.	——— .1606 by .44	———	.365
7.	——— .1606 by 4.4	———	.0365
8.	——— .1606 by 44.	———	.00365
9.	——— 9. by .9	———	10.
10.	——— .9 by 9.	———	.1
11.	——— 186.9 by 7.476	———	25.

Note 1.—When a whole number is to be divided by a greater whole number, cyphers must be affixed to the dividend, as decimal figures.

12.	Divide 3 by 4	Quotient	.75
13.	——— 275 by 3842	———	.071577+
14.	——— 210 by 240	———	.875

Note 2.—When any whole number is divided by another, if there be a remainder, cyphers may be affixed to the dividend, and the quotient continued.

15. Divide 382 by 25 Quotient 15.28
16. ——— 13689 by 75 ——— 182.52
17. ——— 315 by 124 ——— 2.5403+

Division of Decimals may be contracted thus:

Take as many of the left hand figures of the divisor as will be equal to the number of integers and decimals in the quotient, and find how many times they may be had in the first figures of the dividend as usual. Let each remainder be a new dividend; and for every such dividend, leave out one figure to the right hand of the divisor, remembering to carry for the increase of the figures cut off, as in contracted multiplication.

Note.—When there are not so many figures in the divisor as are required to be in the quotient, begin the operation with all the figures, as usual, and continue it till the number of figures in the divisor, and those remaining to be found in the quotient be equal, after which use the contraction.

EXAMPLES.

1. Divide 2508.928065051 by 92.41035, so as to have 4 decimal places in the quotient.

Contracted way.

92.41035)2508.928065051(27.1498
1848207
———
660721
646872
———
13849
9241
———
4608
3696
———
912
832
———
80
72
———
8

Common way.

92.41035)2508.928065051(27.1498
18482070
———
66072106
64687245
———
13848615
9241035
———
46075800
36964140
———
91116605
83169315
———
79472901
73928280
———
5544621

2. Divide 721.17562 by 2.257432, and let there be only 3 places of decimals in the quotient.

Quo. 319.467

3. Divide 12.169825 by 3.14159, so as to have 5 places of decimals in the quotient. Quo. 3.87377

REDUCTION OF DECIMALS.

CASE 1.

To reduce a vulgar fraction to a decimal.

RULE.

Divide the numerator by the denominator.

☞ See examples under note 1, Division of Decimals.

When a compound fraction is given, first reduce it to a single one, and then to a decimal.

EXAMPLES.

1. Reduce $\frac{1}{4}$ to a decimal. Result .25

$$4)1.00$$
$$.25$$

2. Reduce $\frac{1}{2}$ to a decimal. Result .5
3. ——— $\frac{3}{4}$ to a decimal. ——— .75
4. ——— $\frac{3}{8}$ to a decimal. ——— .375
5. ——— $\frac{1}{25}$ to a decimal. ——— .04
6. ——— $\frac{5}{26}$ to a decimal. ——— .1923076+
7. ——— $\frac{1}{2}$ of $\frac{2}{3}$ to a decimal. ——— .333+
8. ——— $\frac{11}{14}$ of $\frac{10}{13}$ to a decimal. ——— .6043956+
9. ——— $\frac{275}{3842}$ to a decimal. ——— .071577+

CASE 2.

To reduce any sum, or quantity, to the decimal of any given denomination.

RULE.

Divide the given sum or quantity, reduced to the lowest denomination mentioned, by the proposed integer, reduced to the same denomination, and the quotient will be the decimal required. Or,

Write the given numbers from the least to the greatest in a perpendicular column, and divide each of them by such a number as will reduce it to the next denomination, annexing the quotient to the succeeding number; the last quotient will be the decimal required.

EXAMPLES.

1. Reduce 17 s. 6 d. to the decimal of a pound.

s. *d.* *d.*	240.)210.000(.875 decimals.
17 6=210	1920
1 L =240	
	1800
Or thus,	1680
12| 6.0	
2|0|17.50|0	1200
	1200
.875 decimal.	

2. Reduce 7 s. 6 d. to the decimal of a pound.
Result .375

3. Reduce 9 d. to the decimal of a pound.
Result .0375

4. Reduce 10 s. $9\frac{1}{2}$ d. to the decimal of a pound.
Result .5385416+

5. Reduce 12 grains to the decimal of a lb. troy.
Result .002083+

6. Reduce 12 drachms to the decimal of a pound avoirdupois. Result .046875

7. Reduce 2 qrs. 14 lb. to the decimal of a cwt.
Result .625

8. Reduce 2 furlongs to the decimal of a league.
Result .0833

9. Reduce 3 qrs. 2 na. to the decimal of a yard.
Result .875

10. Reduce 4 perches to the decimal of an acre.
Result .025

11. Reduce 1 pint to the decimal of a gallon.
Result .125

12. Reduce 7 minutes to the decimal of a day.
Result .00486+

13. Reduce 72 days to the decimal of a year, computing the year at 365 days. Result .1972602+

14. Reduce 52 days to the decimal of a year, computing the year at $365\frac{1}{4}$ days. Result .142368+

15. Reduce $\frac{3}{4}$ d. to the decimal of a shilling.
Result .0625

CASE 3.

To reduce a decimal fraction to its value.

RULE.

Multiply it by the known parts of the integer, and separate to the right of the product as many places as there are places in the given number.

Note.—To find the value of any decimal of a pound by inspection, double the first figure after the point for shillings, adding one thereto if the second be five or more.

Prefix the second figure, if less than five, or its excess above five to the third, and call them so many farthings, abating one when above twelve, and two when above thirty-six.

EXAMPLES.

1. What is the value of .87615 of a L.?

Ans. 17 s. $6\frac{1}{4}$ d.

```
.87615                    By inspection.
    20                       .87615
--------                    --------
17.52300                     17 6 1
    12
--------                  That is,
 6.27600            8×2+1=17 s.        } s.  d.
     4          and 26−1=25 qrs.+6¼  } 17  6¼.
--------
 1.10400
```

2. What is the value of .7854166 of a L.?

Ans. 15 s. $8\frac{1}{2}$ d.

3. What is the value of .76 of a L.?

Ans. 15 s. 2 d. 1.6 qrs.

4. What is the value of .625 of a shilling? Ans. $7\frac{1}{2}$ d.

5. What is the value of .461 of a dollar?

Ans. 46 cts. 1 mill.

6. What is the value of .461 of a shilling?

Ans. 5 d. 2.128 qrs.

7. What is the value of .86 of a cwt.?

Ans. 3 qrs. 12 lb. 5 oz. 1.92 dr.

8. What is the value of .7 of a lb. troy?

Ans. 8 oz. 8 dwt.

9. What is the value of .71 of 4 oz. troy?
Ans. 2 oz. 16 dwt. 19.2 grs.

10. What is the value of .761 of a day?
Ans. 18 h. 15 min. 50.4 sec.

11. What is the value of .67 of a league?
Ans. 2 miles, 0 fur. 3 poles, 1 yd. 3.6 in.

12. What is the value of .712 of a furlong?
Ans. 28 poles, 2 yds. 1 ft. 11.04 in.

13. What is the value of .6875 of a yard?
Ans. 2 qrs. 3 na.

14. What is the value of .3375 of an acre?
Ans. 1 rood, 14 perches.

15. What is the value of .3 of a year?
Ans. 109 days, 12 hours.

16. What is the value of .07 of a barrel of 32 gallons? Ans. 2 gals. 1.92 pts.

17. What is the sum of .48 of a pound, and .16 of a shilling? Ans. 9 s. 9.12 d.

18. What is the sum of .17 of a lb. troy, and .84 of an ounce? Ans. 2 oz. 17 dwt. 14.4 grs.

19. What is the difference between .17 L. and .7 s.?
Ans. 2 s. 8 d. 1.6 qr.

20. What is the difference between .41 day and .16 hour? Ans. 9 h. 40 min. 48 sec.

THE SINGLE RULE OF THREE,

IN DECIMALS.

The operation both in direct and inverse proportion is the same as in whole numbers, regard being had to the right placing of the points.

EXAMPLES.

1. If 2.75 yards of cloth cost 4 L. 13.5 s., what are 12.25 yards worth? Ans. 20 L. 16 s. 6 d.

	yds.		*yds.*		*L.*	*s.*		*L.*	*s.*	*d.*
As	2.75	:	12.25	::	4	13.5	:	20	16	6

2. If 1.4 lb. of mace cost 14.5 s., what cost 75.31 lb.?
Ans. 38 L. 19 s. 11 d. 3.52 qrs.

3. If 1.5 oz. of silver be worth 7.8 s., what is the value of 9.7 lb. Ans. 30 L. 5 s. 3 d. 1.44 qrs.

4. If 1.47 cwt. of sugar be worth 4.5 L., how much is 1.7 lb. worth? Ans. 11.1 d.

5. If 1.6 cwt. of sugar sell for 3 L. 12.76 s., what is the value of 3 hogsheads, each 11 cwt. 3 qrs. 10.12 lb.?
Ans. 80 L. 15 s. 3 d. 3.36 qrs.

6. What is the value of 3 pieces of cloth, each containing 21.5 yds., at 12.3 s. per yard?
Ans. 39 L. 13 s. 4.2 d.

7. If 1 pint of wine cost 1.2 s., what cost 12.5 hogsheads? Ans. 378 L.

8. If 19 yards of linen cost 25.75 dols., what will 435.5 yards come to? Ans. 590.217 dols.+ Or,
590 dols. 21 cts. 7 m.+

9. What will a merchant gain by buying 436 yards of linen, at 8.5 s. per yard, and selling it at 10.75 s. per yard? Ans. 49 L. 1 s.

10. A grocer bought 7.6 cwt. of sugar, at 40.1 s. per cwt. and retailed it out at 4.5 d. per lb. Whether did he gain or lose, and how much?
Ans. He gained 14 s. 5 d. 1.12 qrs.

11. A bought 3 cwt. 1.5 qr. of cloves, at 2.75 s. per lb., which he afterwards sold for 60 L. 11 s. 6 d. How much did he gain by the transaction? Ans. 8 L. 12 s.

12. If 1 yard of ribbon sell for 4.5 cents, how much will 345 yards bring?
Ans. 15.525 dols. Or, $15.52½.

INVERSE PROPORTION.

1. How long will 3 men be in performing a piece of work which will occupy 5 men 40.5 days? Ans. 67.5.

2. How many men can do as much work in .4 of a month, as 16 men can do in 1.5 month? Ans. 60.

3. How much silk .75 of a yard wide, will line 25.5 yards of cloth that is 5 qrs. wide? Ans. 42.5 yds.

4. If a board be .75 of a foot broad, what length must it be to measure 12 square feet? Ans. 16 feet.

5. A had 40.7 yards of linen, for which B gave him 25.6 ells of Holland, at 4.5 s. per ell. How much was the linen per yard? Ans. 2 s. 9 d. 3.84 qrs.

THE DOUBLE RULE OF THREE,

IN DECIMALS.

Questions in this rule are wrought as in whole numbers, placing the points agreeably to former directions.

EXAMPLES.

1. If 3 men receive 8.9 L. for 19.5 days' labor, how much must 20 men have for 100.25 days?

Ans. 305 L. 0 s. 8.2 d.

men 3 : 20 }
days 19.5 : 100.25 days } : : 89 L. : 305 L. 0 s. 8.2 d.

2. If 2 persons receive 4.625 s. for 1 day's labor, how much should 4 persons have for 10.5 days?

Ans. 4 L. 17 s. $1\frac{1}{2}$ d.

3. If the interest of 76.5 L. for 9.5 months be 15.24 L., what sum will gain 6 L. in 12.75 months?

Ans. 22 L. 8 s. $9\frac{3}{4}$ d.

4. How many men will reap 417.6 acres in 12 days, if 5 men reap 52.2 acres in 6 days? Ans. 20 men.

5. If a cellar 22.5 feet long, 17.3 feet wide, and 10.25 feet deep, be dug in 2.5 days, by 6 men, working 12.3 hours a day; how many days of 8.2 hours, should 9 men take to dig another, measuring 45 feet long, 34.6 wide, and 12.3 deep? Ans. 12 days.

INVOLUTION,

OR THE RAISING OF POWERS.

A power is the product arising from multiplying any given number into itself continually a certain number of times; thus,

$2\times2=4$ the second power or square of 2.
$2\times2\times2=8$ the third power or cube of 2.
$2\times2\times2\times2=16$ the fourth power of 2, &c.

The number denoting the power is called the index or exponent of that power.

If two or more powers of the same number are multiplied together, their product is that power whose index is the sum of the exponents of the factors; thus,

$2\times2=4$ the square of 2; $4\times4=16=$4th power of 2; and $16\times16=256=$8th power of 2, &c.

A TABLE OF THE FIRST NINE POWERS.

Roots.	Squares.	Cubes.	4th power.	5th power.	6th power.	7th power.	8th power.	9th power.
1	1	1	1	1	1	1	1	1
2	4	8	16	32	64	128	256	512
3	9	27	81	243	729	2187	6561	19683
4	16	64	256	1024	4096	16384	65536	262144
5	25	125	625	3125	15625	78125	390625	1953125
6	36	216	1296	7776	46656	279936	1679616	10077696
7	49	343	2401	16807	117649	823543	5764801	40353607
8	64	512	4096	32768	262144	2097152	16777216	134217728
9	81	729	6561	59049	531441	4782969	43046721	387420489

EXAMPLES.

1. What is the square of 22? Ans. 484.
2. What is the cube or third power of 4? Ans. 64.

$$4 \times 4 \times 4 = 64.$$

3. What is the fifth power of 7? Ans. 16807.
4. What is the cube or third power of 35? Ans. 42875.
5. What is the fourth power of $\frac{3}{4}$? Ans. $\frac{81}{256}$.
6. What is the cube or third power of .13? Ans. .002197.
7. What is the sixth power of 5.03? Ans. 16196.005304479729

EVOLUTION,

OR THE EXTRACTING OF ROOTS.

The root of a number, or power, is such a number, as being multiplied into itself a certain number of times, will produce that power. Thus 2 is the square root of 4, because $2\times2=4$; and 4 is the cube root of 64, because $4\times4\times4=64$, and so on.

THE SQUARE ROOT.

The square of a number is the product arising from that number multiplied into itself.

Extraction of the square root is the finding of such a number as being multiplied by itself will produce the number proposed.

RULE.

1. Separate the given number into periods of two figures, each, beginning at the units' place.

2. Find the greatest square contained in the left hand period, and set its root on the right of the given number: subtract said square from the left hand period, and to the remainder bring down the next period for a dividual.

3. Double the root for a divisor, and try how often this divisor (with the figure used in the trial thereto annexed) is contained in the dividual: set the number of times in the root: then, multiply and subtract as in division, and bring down the next period to the remainder for a new dividual.

4. Double the ascertained root for a new divisor, and proceed as before, till all the periods are brought down.

Note.—If, when all the periods are brought down, there be a remainder, annex cyphers to the given number, for decimals, and proceed till the root is obtained with a sufficient degree of exactness.

Observe that the decimal periods are to be pointed off from the decimal point towards the right hand; and that there must be as many whole number figures in the root, as there are periods of whole numbers, and as many decimal figures as there are periods of decimals.

PROOF.

Square the root, adding in the remainder, (if any,) and the result will equal the given number.

EXAMPLES.

1. What is the square root of 5499025?

```
 5499025(2345 Ans.
 4                          2345
 ---                        2345
43)149                     ------
   129                      11725
   ---                      9380
464)2090                   7035
    1856                  4690
    ----                 -------
4685)23425                5499025 Proof.
     23425
```

2. What is the square root of 106929? Ans. 327.
3. What is the square root of 451584? Ans. 672.
4. What is the square root of 36372961? Ans. 6031.
5. What is the square root of 7596796? Ans. 2756.228+
6. What is the square root of 3271.4007? Ans. 57.19+
7. What is the square root of 4.372594? Ans. 2.091+
8. What is the square root of 10.4976? Ans. 3.24
9. What is the square root of .00032754? Ans. .01809+
10. What is the square root of 10? Ans. 3.1622+

To extract the Square Root of a Vulgar Fraction.

RULE.

Reduce the fraction to its lowest terms, then extract the square root of the numerator for a new numerator, and the square root of the denominator for a new denominato

Note.—If the fraction be a surd, that is, one whose root can never be exactly found, reduce it to a decimal, and extract the root therefrom.

EXAMPLES.

1. What is the square root of $\frac{7056}{9216}$? Ans. $\frac{7}{8}$
2. What is the square root of $\frac{2704}{4225}$? Ans. $\frac{4}{5}$
3. What is the square root of $\frac{478}{549}$? Ans. .93309+

To extract the Square Root of a Mixed Number.

RULE.

Reduce the mixed number to an improper fraction, and proceed as in the foregoing examples: Or,

Reduce the fractional part to a decimal, annex it to the whole number, and extract the square root therefrom.

EXAMPLES.

1. What is the square root of $37\frac{36}{49}$? Ans. $6\frac{1}{7}$.
2. What is the square root of $27\frac{9}{16}$? Ans. $5\frac{1}{4}$.
3. What is the square root of $85\frac{14}{15}$? Ans. 9.27+
4. What is the square root of $8\frac{5}{7}$? Ans. 2.9519+

APPLICATION.

1. The square of a certain number is 105625: what is that number? Ans. 325.

2. A certain square pavement contains 20736 square stones, all of the same size: what number is contained in one of its sides? Ans. 144.

3. If 484 trees be planted at an equal distance from each other, so as to form a square orchard, how many will be in a row each way? Ans. 22.

4. A certain number of men gave 30 s. 1 d. for a charitable purpose; each man gave as many pence as there were men: how many men were there? Ans. 19.

Note.—The square of the longest side of a right angled triangle is equal to the sum of the squares of the other two sides; and consequently the difference of the square of the longest, and either of the other, is the square of the remaining one.

5. The wall of a certain fortress is 17 feet high, which is surrounded by a ditch 20 feet in breadth; how long must a ladder be to reach from the outside of the ditch to the top of the wall? Ans. 26.24+feet.

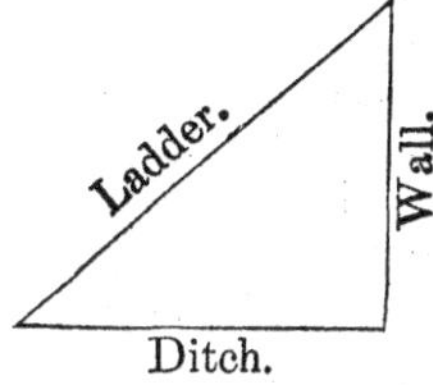

6. A certain castle, which is 45 yards high, is surrounded by a ditch 60 yards broad; what length must a ladder be to reach from the outside of the ditch to the top of the castle? Ans. 75 yards.

7. A line 27 yards long will exactly reach from the top of a fort to the opposite bank of a river, which is known to be 23 yards broad; what is the height of the fort? Ans. 14.142+ yards.

8. Suppose a ladder 40 feet long be so planted as to reach a window 33 feet from the ground, on one side of the street, and without moving it at the foot, will reach a window on the other side 21 feet high; what is the breadth of the street? Ans. 56.64+ feet.

9. Two ships depart from the same port; one of them sails due west 50 leagues, the other due south 84 leagues: how far are they asunder?

Ans. 97.75+ Or, $97\frac{3}{4}$+ leagues.

THE CUBE ROOT.

The cube of a number is the product of that number multiplied into its square.

Extraction of the cube root is the finding of such a number, as, being multiplied into its square, will produce the number proposed.

RULE.

1. Separate the given number into periods of three figures each, beginning at the units place.

2. Find the greatest cube contained in the left hand period, and set its root on the right of the given number: subtract said cube from the left hand period, and to the remainder bring down the next period for a dividual.

3. Square the root and multiply the square by 3 for a defective divisor.

4. Reserve mentally the units and tens of the dividual, and try how often the defective divisor is contained in the rest: place the result of this trial to the root, and its square to the right of said divisor, supplying the place of tens with a cypher, if the square be less than ten.

5. Complete the divisor by adding thereto the product of the last figure of the root by the rest and by 30.

6. Multiply and subtract as in Simple Division, and bring down the next period for a new dividual; for which find a divisor as before, and so proceed till all the periods are brought down.

*** See note under the rule for extracting the square root: it applies equally to this rule.

Note.—Defective divisors, after the first, may be more concisely found thus: To the last complete divisor add the number which completed it with twice the square of the last figure in the root, and the sum will be the next defective divisor.

PROOF.

Involve the root to the third power, adding the remainder, if any, to the result.

EXAMPLES.

1. What is the cube root of 99252.847 ?

```
                                        99252.847(46.3
                                        64
Defective divisor and square of 6=4836)35252
+720=complete divisor             5556)33336
Defective divisor & square of 3=634809)1916847
+4140=complete divisor          638949)1916847
```

2. What is the cube root of 16194277 ? Ans. 253.
3. What is the cube root of 389017 ? Ans. 73.
4. What is the cube root of 5735339 ? Ans. 179.
5. What is the cube root of 34328125 ? Ans. 325.
6. What is the cube root of 22069810125 ? Ans. 280.5
7. What is the cube root of 12.977875 ? Ans. 2.35
8. What is the cube root of 36155.027576 ? Ans. 33.06+
9. What is the cube root of 15926.972504 ? Ans. 25.16+
10. What is the cube root of .001906624 ? Ans. .124

Note 1.—The cube root of a vulgar fraction is found by reducing it to its lowest terms, and extracting the root of the numerator for a numerator, and of the denominator for a denominator. If it be a surd, extract the root of its equivalent decimal.

2. A mixed number may be reduced to an improper fraction, or a decimal, and the root thereof extracted.

1. What is the cube root of $\frac{648}{3000}$? Ans. $\frac{3}{5}$.
2. What is the cube root of $\frac{250}{686}$? Ans. $\frac{5}{7}$.
3. What is the cube root of $\frac{1520}{5130}$? Ans. $\frac{2}{3}$.
4. What is the cube root of $12\frac{19}{27}$? Ans. $2\frac{1}{3}$.
5. What is the cube root of $31\frac{15}{343}$? Ans. $3\frac{1}{7}$.

SURDS.

6. What is the cube root of $7\frac{1}{5}$? Ans. 1.93+
7. What is the cube root of $9\frac{1}{6}$? Ans. 2.092+

APPLICATION.

1. The cube of a certain number is 103823; what is that number? Ans. 47.

2. The cube of a certain number is 1728; what number is it? Ans. 12.

3. There is a cistern or vat of a cubical form which contains 1331 cubical feet; what are the length, breadth, and depth of it? Ans. each 11 feet.

4. A certain stone of a cubical form contains 474552 solid inches; what is the superficial content of one of its sides? Ans. 6084 inches.

A GENERAL RULE FOR EXTRACTING THE ROOTS OF ALL POWERS.

1. Point the given number into periods agreeably to the required root.

2. Find the first figure of the root by the table of powers, or by trial; subtract its power from the left hand period, and to the remainder bring down the first figure in the next period for a dividend.

3. Involve the root to the next inferior power to that which is given, and multiply it by the number denoting the given power, for a divisor; by which find a second figure of the root.

4. Involve the whole ascertained root to the given power, and subtract it from the first and second periods. Bring down the first figure of the next period to the remainder, for a new dividend; to which, find a new divisor, as before; and so proceed.

Note.—The roots of the 4th, 6th, 8th, 9th, and 12th powers, may be obtained more readily thus:

For the 4th root take the square root of the square root.

For the 6th, take the square root of the cube root.

For the 8th, take the square root of the 4th root.

For the 9th, take the cube root of the cube root.

For the 12th, take the cube root of the 4th root.

EXAMPLES.

1. What is the 5th root of 916132832?

```
     916132832(62 Ans.
     7776              6×6×6×6×6=7776
     ------            6×6×6×6×5=6480 divisor.
6480)13853
     ------
     916132832    62×62×62×62×62=916132832
     916132832
     ---------
```

2. What is the fourth root of 140283207936?

Ans. 612.

3. What is the sixth root of 782757789696?

Ans. 96.

4. What is the seventh root of 194754273881?

Ans. 41.

5. What is the ninth root of 1352605460594688?

Ans. 48.

ALLIGATION

Alligation is a rule for adjusting the prices and simples of compound quantities.

CASE 1.

To find the mean price of any part of the composition, when the several quantities and their prices are given.

RULE.

As the sum of the several quantities,
Is to any part of the composition;
So is their total value,
To the value of that part.

PROOF.

The value of the whole mixture at the mean price must agree with the total value of the several quantities at their respective prices.

EXAMPLES.

1. If 6 gallons of wine at 67 cents per gallon; 7 at 80 cents, and 5 at 120 cents per gallon, be mixed together, what will 1 gallon of the mixture be worth?

G.		*cts.*		*cts.*
6	at	67	=	402
7	at	80	=	560
5	at	120	=	600
18				1562

G. *G.* *cts.* *cts.*
As 18 : 1 : : 1562 : 86.77+Answer.

2. If 19 bushels of wheat at 6 s. per bushel; 40 bushels of rye at 4 s. per bushel, and 12 bushels of barley at 3 s. per bushel, be mixed together, what will a bushel of the mixture be worth? Ans. 4 s. $4\frac{1}{4}$ d.

3. If a grocer mix 2 cwt. of sugar at 56 s. per cwt.; 1 cwt. at 43 s. per cwt.; and 2 cwt. at 50 s. per cwt., what will be the value of 1 cwt. of the mixture? Ans. 2 L. 11 s.

4. A farmer mingled 20 bushels of wheat at 5 s. per bushel, and 36 bushels of rye at 3 s. per bushel, with 40 bushels of barley at 2 s. per bushel: I desire to know the worth of a bushel of this mixture. Ans. 3 s.

5. If 4 ounces of silver, worth 75 cents per ounce, be melted with 8 ounces, worth 60 cents per ounce, what will 1 ounce of the mixture be worth? Ans. 65 cts.

6. A wine merchant mixes 12 gallons of wine at 4 s. 10 d. per gallon, with 24 gallons at 5 s. 6 d., and 16 gallons at 6 s. $3\frac{1}{4}$ d.; what is a gallon of the mixture worth? Ans. 5 s. 7 d.

CASE 2.

When the prices of several simples are given, to find how much of each, at their respective rates, must be taken to make a compound or mixture at any proposed price.

RULE.

Set the prices of the simples one under another, and link every price which is not greater than the mean rate, to one or more that *are* greater than that rate; place the difference between each price and the mean rate opposite to the price or prices with which it is linked: then, if only one difference stand opposite to either particular price, it will be the quantity required at that price; but if there be several differences, their sum will be the quantity.

Note.—Different modes of linking will produce different answers.

EXAMPLES.

1. How much rye at 4 s. per bushel, barley at 3 s. per bushel, and oats at 2 s. per bushel, will make a mixture worth 2 s. 6 d. per bushel?

	d.		*bu.* *s.*	
	48	. . . . .	6 at 4	
Mean rate 30	36	. . . . .	6 at 3	Answer.
	24	. 18+6=24	at 2	

2. A vintner has three kinds of wine, viz. one kind at 160 cents per gallon, another at 180 cents, and another at 240 cents; how much of each kind must he take to make a mixture worth 190 cents per gallon?

Ans. { 50 gals. at 160 cts., 50 gals. at 180 cts., and 40 gals. at 240 cts.

3. How much sugar at 4 d. at 6 d. and at 11 d. per lb. must be mixed together to make a composition worth 7 d. per lb.? Ans. an equal quantity of each kind.

4. It is required to mix several sorts of wine, viz. at 9 s., 15 s., and 21 s. per gallon, with water, that the mixture may be worth 12 s. per gallon; how much of each sort must be taken?

Ans. { 3 gals. 9 s., 3 gals. 15 s., and 12 gals. at 21 s. with 9 gals. of water.

5. A grocer has several sorts of sugar, viz. one sort

at 12 cents per lb., another at 11 cents, a third at 9 cents, and a fourth at 8 cents per lb.; how much of each sort must he take to make a mixture worth 10 cents per lb.

	lb. cts.		lb. cts.		lb. cts.
1. Ans.	2 at 12 1 at 11 1 at 9 2 at 8	2. Ans.	3 at 12 2 at 11 2 at 9 3 at 8	3. Ans.	1 at 12 2 at 11 2 at 9 1 at 8
4. Ans.	1 at 12 3 at 11 3 at 9 1 at 8	5. Ans.	3 at 12 1 at 11 3 at 9 2 at 8	6. Ans.	2 at 12 3 at 11 1 at 9 3 at 8

7 Ans. 3 lb. of each sort.

CASE 3.

When the price of all the simples, the quantity of one of them, and the mean price of the whole mixture are given, to find the several quantities of the rest.

RULE.

Link the several prices, and place their differences as in case 2; then,

As the difference opposite to the price of the given quantity,

Is to the differences respectively;

So is the given quantity,

To the several quantities required.

EXAMPLES.

1. A grocer would mix 30 lb. of sugar, at 14 cents per lb., with some at 9 cents, 10 cents, and 13 cents per lb.; how much of each sort must he mix with the thirty lb. that the mixture may sell at 12 cents per lb.?

Mean price, 12	9	 2
	10	 1
	13	 2
	14	 3

	lb. cts.	
As 3 : 2 :: 30 :	20 at 9 per lb.	Answer.
3 : 1 :: 30 :	10 at 10 ——	
3 : 2 :: 30 :	20 at 20 ——	

2. How much barley at 30 cents per bushel, rye at 36 cents, and wheat at 48 cents, must be mixed with 12 bushels of oats, at 18 cents, to make a mixture worth 22 cents per bushel? Ans. 1 bushel of each sort.

3. How much wine at 5 s., at 5 s. 6 d., and at 6 s. per gallon, must be mixed with 3 gallons, at 4 s. per gallon, so that the mixture may be worth 5 s. 4 d. per gallon?

Ans. 3 gals. at 5 s., 6 at 5 s. 6 d., and 6 at 6 s.

4. How much tea at 12 s., 10 s., and at 6 s. per lb., must be mixed with 20 pounds, at 4 s. per lb., to make a mixture worth 8 s. per lb.?

Ans. 10 lb. at 6 s., 10 lb. at 10 s., and 20 lb. at 12 s.

CASE 4.

When the prices of the several simples, the quantity to be compounded, and the mean price are given, to find the quantity of each simple.

RULE.

Link the several prices, and place their differences as before; then,

As the sum of the differences,
Is to the difference opposite to each price;
So is the quantity to be compounded,
To the quantity required.

EXAMPLES.

1. How much sugar at 10 cents, 12 cents, and 15 cents, per lb., will be required to make a mixture of 20 lb. worth 13 cents per lb.?

13.	10	- 2	As 8 : 2 : : 20 :	5 lb. at 10cts.	Ans.
	12	- 2	8 : 4 : : 20 :	10 lb. at 15cts.	
	15	3+1=4	8 : 2 : : 20 :	5 lb. at 12cts.	
		8 Sum of differences.			

2. A brewer has three sorts of beer, viz., at 10 d., 8 d., and 6 d. per gallon; how much of each sort must he take to make a mixture of 30 gallons, worth 7 d. per gallon?

Ans. 5 gals. at 10 d., 5 gals. at 8 d., and 20 gals. at 6 d.

3. A goldsmith has gold of 15, 17, 20, and 22 carats fine, and would melt together of each of these so much as to make a mass of 40 oz. of 18 carats fine; how much of each sort is necessary?

Ans. { 16 oz. of 15 carats, 8 oz. of 17 carats, 4 oz. of 20 carats, and 12 oz. of 22 carats fine.

4. How many gallons of water must be mixed with wine, at 4 s. per gallon, so as to fill a vessel of 80 gallons, that may be afforded at 2 s. 9 d. per gallon?

Ans. 25 gallons of water, with 55 of wine.

POSITION.

Position is a rule for finding an unknown number, by one or more supposed numbers. It is divided into two parts, single and double.

SINGLE POSITION.

Single Position teaches to resolve such questions as require only one supposition.

RULE.

Suppose any number to be the true one, and proceed with it agreeably to the tenor of the question; then,

As the result of the operation,
Is to the number given;
So is the supposed number,
To the number sought.

PROOF.

Work with the answer according to the tenor of the question, and the result must equal the given number.

EXAMPLES.

1. A, B, and C bought a quantity of wine for 340 dollars, of which sum A paid three times more than B, and B four times more than C; how much did each pay?

	$		$	
Suppose A paid	36	A paid	240	Ans.
Then B paid	12	B paid	80	
And C paid	3	C paid	20	
	51		340	Proof.

As 51 : 340 : : 36 : 240 sum paid by A.

2. A person after spending $\frac{1}{3}$ and $\frac{1}{4}$ of his money, had 60 L. left; how much had he at first? Ans. 144 L.

3. What number of dollars is that, of which the $\frac{1}{4}$, $\frac{1}{5}$, and $\frac{1}{6}$, make 74? Ans. 120.

4. A person having about him a certain number of crowns, said, if a third, a fourth, and a sixth of them were added together, the sum would be 45; how many crowns had he? Ans. 60.

5. What is the age of a person who says, that if $\frac{3}{5}$ of the years I have lived be multiplied by 7, and $\frac{2}{3}$ of them be added to the product, the sum will be 292?

Ans. 60 years.

6. A schoolmaster being asked how many scholars he had, answered, if to double the number I add $\frac{1}{2}$, $\frac{1}{3}$, and $\frac{1}{4}$ of them, I shall have 333; how many had he?

Ans. 108.

7. A certain sum of money is to be divided among 4 persons in such a manner that the first shall have $\frac{1}{3}$ of it, the second $\frac{1}{4}$, the third $\frac{1}{6}$, and the fourth the remainder, which is 28 dollars; what is the sum?

Ans. 112 dollars.

8. What sum, at 6 per cent. per annum, will amount to 860 L. in 12 years? Ans. 500 L.

DOUBLE POSITION.

Double Position teaches to find the true number, by making use of two supposed numbers.

RULE.

Suppose two numbers, and work with each agreeably to the tenor of the question, noting the errors of the results: multiply the errors of each operation into the supposed number of the other; then,

If the errors be alike, *i. e.*, both too much, or both too little, take their difference for a divisor, and the difference of the products for a dividend: but if the errors be unlike, take their sum for a divisor, and the sum of the products for a dividend.

PROOF.

As in Single Position.

EXAMPLES.

1. A, B, and C would divide 80 dollars among them in such a manner, that B may have 5 dollars more than A, and C 10 dollars more than B; required the share of each?

Suppose A's share	$10	Suppose A's share	$15
B's ——	15	B's ——	20
C's ——	25	C's ——	30
	50		65

80−50=30 error too little. 80−65=15 error too little.

Errors.	Er. Sup.	
30	30×15=450	
15	15×10=150	Ans. A 20, B 25, C 35
15 diff. of er.	15)300 diff. of prod.	80
	20 A's share.	

2. D, E, and F would divide 100 L. among them, so as that E may have 3 L. more than D, and F 4 L. more than E; what is the share of each?

Ans. D's share 30 L., E's 33 L., F's 37 L.

3. A, B, and C owe 1000 L., of which B is to pay 100 L. more than A, and C is to pay as much as both A and B; how much is each man's share of the debt?

Ans. A's share is 200 L., B's 300 L., and C's 500 L.

4. Bought linen at 4 s. per yard, and muslin at 2 s. per yard; the number of yards of both was 8, and the whole cost 20 s.; how many yards were there of each?

Ans. 2 yards of linen, and 6 yards of muslin.

5. The head of a certain fish is 9 inches long; its tail is as long as its head and half of its body; and the length of its body is equal to the length of its head and tail: what is the whole length? Ans. 6 feet.

6. A laborer hired for 40 days upon this condition, that he should receive 20 cents for every day he wrought, and should forfeit 10 cents for every day he was idle; at settlement he received 5 dollars. How many days did he work, and how many days was he idle? Ans. Wrought 30 days, idle 10.

7. A father, dying, left to his three sons, A, B, and C, his estate in money, dividing it as follows, viz.: to A he gave half the estate, wanting 44 L.; to B he gave a third of it, and 14 L. over; and to C he gave the remainder, which was 82 L. less than the share of B. What was the whole sum left, and what was each son's share?

Ans. { The sum left was 588 L., of which A had 250 L., B 210 L., and C 128 L.

8. Two persons, A and B, both have the same income; A saves one-fifth of his every year; but B, by spending 150 dollars per annum more than A, at the end of 8 years finds himself 400 dollars in debt: what is their income, and what does each spend per annum?

Ans. { Their income is 500 dollars per annum.
A spends 400 dols., and B 550.

ARITHMETICAL PROGRESSION.

Any rank or series of numbers, increasing or decreasing by a common difference, is said to be in arithmetical progression; as 2, 4, 6, 8, 10, and 6, 5, 4, 3, 2, 1.

The numbers which form the series are called the *terms*. The first and last terms are called the *extremes*.

Note.—In any series of numbers in Arithmetical Progression, the sum of the two extremes is equal to the sum of any two terms equally distant from them; as in the latter of the above series $6+1=4+3$, and $=5+2$.

When the number of terms is odd, the double of the middle term is equal to the sum of the two extremes, or any two terms equally distant from the middle term; as in the former of the foregoing series $6\times2=2+10$, and $=4+8$.

CASE 1.

The first term, common difference, and number of terms given, to find the last term, and sum of all the terms.

RULE.

1. Multiply the number of terms, less 1, by the common difference, and to the product add the first term, the sum is the last term.

2. Multiply the sum of the two extremes by the number of terms, and half the product will be the sum of all the terms.

EXAMPLES.

1. The first term of a certain series in arithmetical progression is 2, the common difference is 2, and the

number of terms 15; what is the last term, and the sum of all the terms?

15	number of terms.	30	two extremes.
1		2	
14	number of terms less 1.	32	
2	common difference.	15	number of terms.
28		160	
2	first term.	32	
30	last term.	2)480	
		240	Sum of all the terms.

2. Bought 15 yards of linen, at 2 cents for the first yard, 4 for the second, 6 for the third, &c., increasing 2 cents every yard; what was the cost of the last yard, and what was the cost of the whole?

Ans. The last yard cost 30 cts., the whole cost $2.40.

3. Sold 20 yards of silk, at 3 d. for the first yard, 6 d. for the second, 9 d. for the third, &c., increasing 3 d. every yard; what sum did it amount to?

Ans. 2 L. 12 s. 6 d.

4. Sixteen persons gave charity to a poor man; the first gave 5 d., the second 9 d., and so on in an arithmetical progression; how much did the last person give, and what sum did the man receive?

Ans. The last gave 5 s. 5 d., sum received, 2 L. 6 s. 8 d.

5. If 100 stones be laid two yards distant from each other in a right line, and a basket placed two yards from the first stone; what distance must a person travel to gather them singly into the basket?

Ans. 11 miles, 3 fur. 180 yds.

6. A merchant sold 1000 yards of linen, at 2 pins for the first yard, 4 for the second, and 6 for the third, &c., increasing two pins every yard; how much did the linen produce, when the pins were afterwards sold at 12 for a farthing? Ans. 86 L. 17 s. 10 d.

CASE 2.

When the two extremes and number of terms are given, to find the common difference.

RULE.

Divide the difference of the extremes by the number of terms, less one; the quotient will be the common difference.

EXAMPLES.

1. Twenty and sixty are the two extremes of a certain series in arithmetical progression, and 21 is the number of terms; what is the common difference?

Ans 2.

60 }
20 } extremes.

21—1=20)40 Difference of extremes.

2 Common difference.

2. There are 21 men whose ages are equally distant from each other in arithmetical progression: the youngest is 20 years old, and the eldest 60; what is the common difference of their ages, and the age of each man?

Ans. Common difference 2 years.
60 years is the age of the first man.
60—2=58 - - - - age of the second.
58—2=56 - - - - age of the third, &c.

3. A debt is to be paid at 16 different payments in arithmetical progression; the first payment to be 14 L. and the last 100 L.: what is the common difference, each payment, and the whole debt?

Ans. { Common difference 5 L. 14 s. 8 d. First payment 14 L. Second, 19 L. 14 s. 8 d. Third, 25 L. 9 s. 4 d. &c.

4. A person is to travel from Philadelphia to a certain place in 16 days, and to go but 4 miles the first day, increasing every day by an equal excess, so that the last day's journey may be 79 miles; what is the common difference; and what the whole distance?

Ans. { Common difference 5 miles. Distance 664 miles.

GEOMETRICAL PROGRESSION.

Any series of numbers, the terms of which increase by a common multiplier, or decrease by a common divisor, are said to be in geometrical progression; as 3, 6, 12, 24, 48; and 48, 24, 12, 6, 3.

The multiplier or divisor by which the series is increased or decreased is called the *ratio.*

The last term and sum of the series is found by this

RULE.

1. Raise the ratio to the power whose index is one less than the number of terms given, which, being multiplied by the first term, will give the last term, or greater extreme.

2. Multiply the last term by the ratio, from the product subtract the first term, and divide the remainder by ratio less one for the sum of the series.

EXAMPLES.

1. A thresher wrought 20 days, and received for the first day's labor 4 grains of wheat; for the second, 12; for the third, 36, &c. How much did his wages amount to, allowing 7680 grains to make a pint, and the whole to be disposed of at one dollar per bushel?

Note.—The first term in this question is 4, the ratio 3, the number of terms 20: therefore raise the ratio to the 19th power, which is one less than the number of terms.

1st power. 2d power. 3d power. 4th power.

```
Ratio 3, 9, 27, 81
                81
               ---
                81
               648
               ---
              6561  8th power of the ratio.
              6561
              ----
              6561
            39366
           32805
          39366
          --------
          43046721  16th power.
                27  3d power.
         ---------
         301327047
         86093442
        ----------
        1162261467  19th power.
                 4  1st term.
        ----------
        4649045868
                 3  Ratio.
       -----------
       13947137604
                 4  First term.
       -----------
Ratio less one 2)13947137600
       -----------
   7680)6973568800  Sum of the series.
        ----------
          908016 pints, = 14187 bushels.
```

14187 bushels, at 1 dol. p. bu. amount to 14187 dols. Ans.

2. Sold 24 yards of Holland, at 2 d. for the first yard, 4 d. for the second, 8 d. for the third, &c.; how much did it amount to? Ans. 139810 L. 2 s. 6 d

3. Bought 30 bushels of wheat, at 2 d. for the first bushel, 4 d. for the second, 8 d. for the third, &c.; what does the whole amount to, and what is the price per bushel on an average?

Ans. { 8947848 L. 10 s. 6 d. Amount.
298261 L. 12 s. 4 d. per bushel.

4. A merchant sold 30 yards of lace, at 2 pins for the first yard, 6 for the second, 18 for the third, &c., and disposed of the pins at 1000 for a farthing; how much did he receive for the lace? and how much did he gain by the sale, supposing the lace cost him 100 L. per yd.?

Ans. { Received 214469929 L. 5 s. $3\frac{1}{2}$ d.
Gained 214466929 L. 5 s. $3\frac{1}{2}$ d.

5. A goldsmith sold 1 lb. of gold, at a farthing for the first ounce, a penny for the second, 4 d. for the third, &c., in quadruple proportion; how much did he receive for the whole, and how much did he gain by the sale, supposing he gave 4 L. per ounce for the gold?

Ans. { He received 5825 L. 8 s. $5\frac{1}{4}$ d.
And gained 5777 L. 8 s. $5\frac{1}{4}$ d.

6. What sum would purchase a horse with 4 shoes, and eight nails in each shoe, at one farthing for the first nail, a halfpenny for the second, a penny for the third, &c. doubling to the last? Ans. 4473924 L. 5 s. $3\frac{3}{4}$ d.

7. A person married his daughter on new year's day, and gave her one dollar towards her portion, promising to double it on the first day of every month for one year; what was her portion? Ans. 4095 dols.

8. Suppose a man wrought 20 days, and received for the first day's labor 4 grains of corn, for the second 12, for the third 36, &c.; what did he receive for his labor, supposing 7680 grains to make a pint, and the whole to be sold at 2 s. 6 d. per bushel?

Ans. 1773 L. 7 s. 6 d.

COMPOUND INTEREST,

BY DECIMALS.

The ratio in compound interest is the amount of one pound or dollar for one year; which is thus found:

As 100 : 1 :: 105 : 1.05. As 100 : 1 :: 105.5 : 1.055.

For quarterly amounts, take the 4th root of the ratio; for half yearly, the square root; and, for 3 quarters, the product of the quarterly and half yearly.

Thus, $\sqrt[4]{1.03}=1.007417$; $\sqrt[2]{1.03}=1.014889$; and $1.007417\times1.014889=1.022416$, for 3 quarters.

TABLE 1.

Rate per cent.	*Amounts of* 1 *L. for a year and for quarters, at Compound Interest.*				Simp. Int. of 1 *L.* for 1 month.
	Ratio.	For 3 qrs.	For 2 qrs.	For 1 qr.	
3	1.03	1.022416	1.014889	1.007417	.002500
3½	1.035	1.026137	1.017349	1.008637	.002917
4	1.04	1.029852	1.019804	1.009853	.003333
4½	1.045	1.033563	1.022252	1.011065	.003750
5	1.05	1.037270	1.024695	1.012272	.004167
5½	1.055	1.040973	1.027132	1.013475	.004583
6	1.06	1.044671	1.029536	1.014674	.005000
6½	1.065	1.048364	1.031988	1.015868	.005417
7	1.07	1.052053	1.034408	1.017058	.005833

The ratio involved to the time is the amount of 1 L. or dollar for the time given; as a square for 2 years, a cube for 3, &c.; thus, $1.06 \times 1.06 \times 1.06 \times 1.06$.

or $1.06^4 = 1.262477$ = the 4th power of 1.06, or the ratio involved to 4 years.

When the ratio is to be involved to years and quarters, the power for the years is to be multiplied by the proper quarterly amount; as, $1.262477 \times 1.044671 = 1.318873$ for $4\frac{3}{4}$ years, &c.

The power or the amount of 1 L. or dollar may also be obtained for months and days (nearly) by adding the monthly simple interest of 1 L. or dollar, or proper parts thereof, to the amount of the quarter next preceding the expiration of the given time, for what that time exceeds the said quarter; thus,

Amount for $\frac{1}{2}$ yr. =	1.029563 :	For $4\frac{3}{4}$ yrs. =	1.318873
Int. of 1 L. for 1 mo. =	.005000	————	.005000
One sixth for 5 dys. =	.000833	————	.000833

For 7 mo. 5 dys. = 1.035396 : For 4 years, 10 mo. 5 dys. = 1.324706.

The ratio may be thus involved to any time whatever; but the operation is facilitated by the following tables; which may be extended to 100 years, or upwards, by multiplying the amount for 46, by that for the time above 46, &c.

TABLE II. Showing the amount of 1 *L.* or Dollar from 1 year to 46.

Y.	3½ per cent.	4 per cent.	4½ per cent.	5 per cent.	5½ per cent.	6 per cent.
1	1.0350000	1.0400000	1.0450000	1.0500000	1.0550000	1.0600000
2	1.0712250	1.0816000	1.0920250	1.1025000	1.1130250	1.1360000
3	1.1087178	1.1248640	1.1411661	1.1576950	1.1742413	1.1910160
4	1.1475230	1.1698585	1.1925186	1.2155062	1.2388246	1.2624769
5	1.1876863	1.2166529	1.2461819	1.2762815	1.3069598	1.3382256
6	1.2292553	1.2653190	1.3022601	1.3400956	1.3788426	1.4185191
7	1.2722792	1.3159317	1.3608618	1.4071004	1.4546789	1.5036302
8	1.3168090	1.3685690	1.4221006	1.4774554	1.5346862	1.5938480
9	1.3628973	1.4233118	1.4860951	1.5513282	1.6190939	1.6894789
10	1.4105987	1.4802442	1.5529694	1.6238946	1.7081440	1.7908476
11	1.4599697	1.5394540	1.6228530	1.7103393	1 8020919	1.8982985
12	1.5110686	1.6010322	1.6958814	1.7958563	1.9012069	2.0121964
13	1.5630560	1.6650735	1.7721961	1.8856491	2.0057732	2.1329282
14	1.6186945	1.7316764	1.8519449	1.9799316	2.1160907	2.2609039
15	1.6753488	1.8009435	1.9352824	2.0789281	2.2324756	2 3965581
16	1.7339860	1.8729812	2.0223701	2.1828745	2.3552617	2.5403517
17	1.7946755	1.9479005	2.1133768	2.2920183	2.4848011	2.6927727
18	1.8574892	2.0258161	2.2084787	2.4066192	2.6214652	2.8543391
19	1.9225013	2.1068491	2.3078603	2.5269502	2.7656458	3.0255995
20	1.9897888	2.1911231	2.4117140	2.6532977	2.9177563	3.2071355
21	2.0594314	2.2787680	2.5202411	2.7859625	3.0782329	3.3995636
22	2.1315115	2.3699187	2.6336520	2.9252607	3.2475357	3.6035374
23	2.2061144	2.4647155	2.7521663	3.0715237	3.4261502	3.8097496
24	2.2833284	2.5633041	2.8760138	3.2250999	3.6145885	4.0489346
25	2.3632449	2.6658363	3.0054344	3.3863549	3.8133910	4.2918707
26	2.4459985	2.7724697	3.1406790	3.5556726	4.0231279	4.5493829
27	2.5315671	2.8833685	3.2820095	3.7334563	4.2443999	4.8223459
28	2.6201719	2.9987033	3.4296999	3.9201291	4.4778419	5.1116867
29	2.7118779	3.1186514	3.5840364	4.1161356	4.7241232	5.4183870
30	2.8067937	3.2433975	3.7453181	4.3219423	4.9839469	5.7434912
31	2.9050314	3.3731334	3.9138574	4.5380394	5.2580671	6.0881007
32	3.0067075	3 5080587	4.0899810	4.7649414	5.5472608	6.4533867
33	3.1119423	3.6481831	4.2740301	5.0031885	5.8523600	6.8405899
34	3.2208603	3.7943163	4.4663015	5.2533479	6.1742398	7.2510253
35	3.3335904	3.9460889	4.6673478	5.5160152	6.5138230	7.6860868
36	3.4502661	4.1030325	4.8773784	5.7918101	6.8720832	8.1472520
37	3.5710254	4.2680898	5.0068604	6.0814069	7.2500478	8.6360871
38	3.6960113	4.4388134	5.3262192	6.3854772	7.6488004	9.1542523
39	3.8253717	4.6163659	5.5658990	6.7047511	8.0694844	9.7035074
40	3.9592597	4.8010206	5.8163645	7.0399887	8.5133060	10.2857178
41	4.0978337	4.9930614	6.0781009	7.3919881	8.9815378	10.9028608
42	4.2412579	5.1927838	6.3514240	7.7615871	9.4755224	11.5570325
43	4.3897020	5.4004952	6.6375523	8.1496669	9.9966761	12.2504547
44	4.5433415	5.6165150	6.9362421	8.5571502	10.5464933	12.9854817
45	4.7023585	5.8411756	7.2483730	8.9850077	11.1265504	13.7646107
46	4.8669411	6.0748236	7.5745497	9.4342581	11.7385217	14.5904873

CASE 1.

The principal, time, and rate given, to find the amount, or interest.

RULE.

Multiply the principal by the ratio involved to the time, (found either by involution, or in table II.) and the product will be the amount; from which subtract the principal, for the compound interest.

EXAMPLES.

1. What will 225 L. amount to in 3 years, at 5 per cent. per annum?

$1.05 \times 1.05 \times 1.05 = 1.157625$ raised to the third power; then, $1.157625 \times 225 = 260$ L. 9 s. 3 d. 3 qrs. the Ans.

2. What will 480 L. amount to in 6 years, at 5 per cent. per annum? Ans. 643 L. 4 s. 11.0178 d.

3. What is the amount of 500 L. at $4\frac{1}{4}$ per cent. per annum, for 4 years? Ans. 590 L. 11 s. 5 d. 2.95+qrs.

4. What is the compound interest of a bond for 764 dollars, for 4 years and 9 months, at 6 per cent. per annum? Ans. 243 dols. 61 cts.+

CASE 2.

DISCOUNT,

Or, the amount, rate, and time given, to find the principal:

RULE.

Divide the amount by the ratio involved to the time.

EXAMPLES.

1. What principal must be put to interest, to amount to 260 L. 9 s. 3 d. 3 qrs. in 3 years, at 5 per cent. per annum?

260 L. 9 s. 3 d. 3 qrs. = 260.465625 L.

$1.05 \times 1.05 \times 1.05 = 1.157625$ ratio raised to the 3d power.

1.157625)260.465625(225 L. Ans.

2. What principal will amount to 547 L. 9 s. 10 d. 2.0528 qrs. in 5 years, at 4 per cent. per annum? Ans. 450 L.

3. What principal will amount to 619 L. 8 s. 2 d. 3.809 qrs. in 4 years, at $5\frac{1}{2}$ per cent.? Ans. 500 L.

An annuity is a sum of money payable yearly, half yearly, or quarterly, for a number of years, during life, or for ever; and may draw interest if it remain unpaid after it becomes due.

Tables to facilitate the calculations of Annuities.

TABLE III. Showing the amount of 1 *L.* annuity.

Y.	4 per cent.	4½ per cent.	5 per cent.	5½ per cent.	6 per cent.	Y.
1	1.	1.	1.	1.	1.	1
2	2.04	2.045	2.05	2.055	2.06	2
3	3.1216	3.137025	3.1525	3.168225	3.1836	3
4	4.246464	4.278191	4.310125	4.342266	4.374602	4
5	5.416322	5.47071	5.525631	5.581091	5.637093	5
6	6.632975	6.716892	6.801913	6.888051	6.975318	6
7	7.898294	8.019152	8.142008	8.266894	8.393837	7
8	9.214226	9.380014	9.549109	9.721573	9.897468	8
9	10.582795	10.802114	11.026564	11.256259	11.491316	9
10	12.006107	12.28821	12.577892	12.875354	13.180795	10
11	13.486351	13.841179	14.206787	14.583498	14.971643	11
12	15.025805	15.464032	15.917126	16.38559	16.869942	12
13	16.626838	17.159913	17.712983	18.286798	18.882138	13
14	18.291911	18.932109	19.598632	20.292572	21.015066	14
15	20.023588	20.784054	21.578563	22.408663	23.275971	15
16	21.824531	22.719337	23.657492	24.64114	25.672528	16
17	23.697512	24.741707	25.840366	26.996402	28.212881	17
18	25.645413	26.855084	28.132385	29.481205	30.905653	18
19	27.671229	29.063562	30.539004	32.102671	33.759993	19
20	29 778078	31.371423	33.065954	34.868318	36.785592	20
21	31.969202	33.783137	35.719252	37.786075	39.992728	21
22	34.247970	36.833378	38.505214	40.864309	43.392291	22
23	36.617888	38.93703	41.430475	44.111846	46.995828	23
24	39.082604	41.689196	44.501999	47.537998	50.815578	24
25	41.645908	44.56521	47.727099	51.152588	54.864513	25
26	44.311745	47.570645	51.113454	54.965979	59.156383	26
27	47.084214	50.711324	54.669126	58.989109	63.705766	27
28	49.967582	53.993333	58.402583	63.23351	68.528117	28
29	52.966286	57.423033	62.322712	67.711353	73.639798	29
30	56.084938	61.007069	66.438847	72.435478	79.058186	30
31	59.328335	64.752388	70.76079	77.419429	84.801677	31
32	62.701469	68.666245	75.298829	82.677498	90.889778	32
33	66.209527	72.756226	80.063771	88.22476	97.343165	33
34	69.857904	77.030256	85.066959	94.077122	104.183754	34
35	73.652225	81.496618	90.320307	100.251363	111.434780	35
36	77.598314	86.163966	95.836323	106.765188	119.120867	36
37	81.702246	91.041344	101.628139	113.637274	127.268118	37
38	85.970336	96.138205	107.709546	120.887324	135.904206	38
39	90.40915	101.464424	114.095023	128.536127	145.058458	39
40	95.025516	107.030329	120.799774	136.605146	154.761966	40

TABLE IV.

Showing the present worth of 1 *L.* annuity for any number of years, from 1 to 40.

Y.	4 per cent.	4½ per cent.	5 per cent.	5½ per cent.	6 per cent.	Y.
1	0.96154	0.95694	0.95231	0.94786	0.94339	1
2	1.88609	1.87267	1.85941	1.81632	1.83339	2
3	2.77509	2.74876	2.72325	2.69793	2.67301	3
4	3.62989	3.58752	3.54595	3.50514	3.4651	4
5	4.45182	4.38997	4.32988	4.27028	4.21236	5
6	5.24214	5.15787	5.07569	4.99553	4.91732	6
7	6.40205	5.8927	5.78637	5.68297	5.58238	7
8	6.73274	6.59589	6.46321	6.33457	6.20979	8
9	7.43533	7.26879	7.10782	6.95220	6.80169	9
10	8.11089	7.91272	7.72173	7.53762	7.36008	10
11	8.76048	8.52892	8 3064	8.09254	7.88687	11
12	9.38500	9.11858	8.86325	8.61852	8.38384	12
13	9.98565	9.68285	9.39357	9.11708	8.85268	13
14	10.56312	10.22282	9.89864	9.58965	9.29498	14
15	11.41839	10.73954	10.37965	10.03759	9.71225	15
16	11.65229	11.23401	10.83777	10.46216	9.10589	16
17	12.16567	11.70719	11.27407	10.86461	10.47726	17
18	12.65929	12.15999	11.68958	11.24607	10.8276	18
19	13.13394	12.59329	12.08532	11.60765	11.15811	19
20	13.59032	13.00793	12.46221	11.93034	11.46992	20
21	14.02916	13.40472	12.82115	12.27524	11.76407	21
22	14.45111	13.78442	13.163	12.58317	12.04158	22
23	14.85684	14.14777	13.48857	12.87504	12.30338	23
24	15.24696	14.49548	13.79864	13.15170	12.55035	24
25	15.62208	14.82821	14.09384	13.41391	12.78335	25
26	15.98277	15.14661	14.37518	13.66250	13.00316	26
27	16.32959	15.45130	14.64303	13.89810	13.21053	27
28	16.66306	15.74287	14.89813	14.12142	13.40616	28
29	16.98371	16.02189	15.14107	14.33310	13.59072	29
30	17.29203	16.28889	15.37245	14.53375	13.76483	30
31	17.58849	16.54439	15.59281	14.72393	13.92908	31
32	17.87355	16.78889	15.80268	14.90420	14.08404	32
33	18.14764	17.02286	16.00255	15.07507	14.23023	33
34	18.41126	17.24676	16.1929	15.23703	14.36814	34
35	18.66461	17.46101	16.37419	15.39055	14.49825	35
36	18.90828	17.66604	16.54685	15.53607	14.62098	36
37	19.14258	17.86224	16.71129	15.67400	14.73678	37
38	19.36786	18.04999	16.86789	15.80474	14.84602	38
39	19.58448	18.22965	17.01704	15.92866	14.94907	39
40	19.79277	18.40158	17.15909	16.04612	14.92640	40

TABLE V.

Rate per ct.	Half yearly payments.	Quarterly payments.
3	1.007445	1.011181
$3\frac{1}{2}$	1.008675	1.013031
4	1.009902	1.014877
$4\frac{1}{2}$	1.101126	1.016720
5	1.012348	1.018559
$5\frac{1}{2}$	1.013567	1.020395
6	1.014781	1.022257
$6\frac{1}{2}$	1.015993	1.024055
7	1.017204	1.025880

The construction of this table is from an algebraic theorem, given by the learned A. de Moivre, in his treatise of Annuities on Lives, which may be in words, thus :

For half yearly payments take a unit from the ratio, and from the square root of the ratio; half the quotient of the first remainder divided by the latter, will be the tabular number.

For quarterly payments use the 4th root as above, and take one quarter of the quotient.

CASE 1.

The annuity, time, and rate of interest given, to find the amount.

RULE.

From the ratio involved to the time take a unit, or one, for the dividend; which divide by the ratio less one; and multiply the quotient by the annuity, for the amount or answer. Or, by Table III.

Multiply the number under the rate, and opposite to the time, by the annuity, and the product will be the amount for yearly payments.

If the payments be half yearly or quarterly, the amount for the given time, found as above, multiplied by the proper number in Table V., will be the true amount.

EXAMPLES.

1. What will an annuity of 50 L. per annum, payable yearly, amount to in 4 years at 5 per cent.?

$1.05 \times 1.05 \times 1.05 \times 1.05 - 1 = .21550625$

$1.05 - 1 = .05).21550625$

4.310125
50

Ans. L. 215.506250 = 215 L. 10 s. 1 d. 2 qrs.

2. What will an annuity of 30 L. per annum, payable yearly, amount to in 4 years, at 5 per cent. per annum, and what would be the respective amounts, if the payments were to be half yearly or quarterly?

Ans. { Amount for yearly payments is L. 129.30375
—— for half yearly —— L. 130.9004
—— for quarterly —— L. 131.7035 }

If a salary of 35 L. per annum, to be paid yearly, be omitted for 6 years at $5\frac{1}{2}$ per cent., what is the amount? Ans. 241 L. 1 s. 7 d. 2.5 + qrs.

CASE 2.

The annuity, time, and rate given, to find the present worth.

RULE.

Divide the annuity by the ratio involved to the time, and subtract the quotient from the annuity; divide the remainder by the ratio less one, and the quotient will be the present worth; or, by Table IV.

Multiply the number under the rate, and opposite the time by the annuity, and the product will be the present worth.

When the payments are half yearly or quarterly, multiply the present worth so found, by the proper number in Table V.

EXAMPLES.

1. What is the present worth of a pension of 30 L. per annum for 5 years, at 4 per cent.?

Ans. 133 L. 11 s. 1 d.

Number from Table IV. 4.45182
×30 annuity.

L. 133.55460

Or, 133 L. 11 s. 1.104 d.

2. What is the present worth of 20 L. a year for 6 years, payable either yearly, half yearly, or quarterly, computing at 5 per cent. per annum?

L.

Ans. { Present worth for yearly payments, 101.5138
—— for half yearly —— 102.7673
—— for quarterly —— 103.3978 }

3. What is the yearly rent of 50 L. to continue 5 years, worth in ready money, at 5 per cent.?

Ans. 216 L. 9 s. 10 d. 2.24 qrs.

ANNUITIES TAKEN IN REVERSION,

AT COMPOUND INTEREST.

Annuities taken in reversion, are certain sums of money payable yearly for a limited period, but not to commence till after the expiration of a certain time.

CASE 1.

The annuity, time of reversion, time of continuance, and rate given, to find the present worth of the annuity in reversion.

RULE.

Divide the annuity by the ratio involved to the time of continuance, and subtract the quotient from the annuity for a dividend; multiply the ratio involved to the time of reversion by the ratio, less one, for a divisor; the quotient of this division will be the present worth. Or,

Take two numbers under the given rate in Table IV., viz., that opposite the sum of the two given times, and that against the time of reversion, and multiply their difference by the annuity of the present worth.

When the payments are half yearly or quarterly, use Table V.

EXAMPLES.

1. What is the present worth of a reversion of a lease of 40 L. per annum, to continue for six years, but not to commence till the end of 2 years, allowing 6 per cent. to the purchaser?

40 annuity.

Ration involved to the time. } =1.4185191)40.000000000000(28.19842

11.80158

1.06×1.06×.06=.067416)11.80158(175.056+L. Ans.

Or by Table IV. First, the sum of the two given

times is 8 years, and the time of reversion 2 years; therefore,

Take for 8 years 6.20979
—— for 2 do. 1.83339

Difference 4.37640
× 40 annuity.
L. 175.05600 Ans. as before.

2. A person owns a farm which he proposes to let for 8 years, at 100 dollars per annum; but cannot give possession till after the expiration of two years; what is the present worth of such a lease, allowing 4 per cent. for present payment? Ans. 622.48 dols.

3. What is the present worth of a reversion of a lease of 60 L. per annum, to continue 7 years, but not to commence till the end of 3 years, allowing 5 per cent. to the purchaser? Ans. 299 L. 18 s. 2.112 d.

PERPETUITIES,

AT COMPOUND INTEREST.

Perpetuities are such annuities as continue forever.

CASE 1.

The annuity, and given rate, to find the present worth.

RULE.

Divide the annuity by the ratio less one, for the present worth.

Note.—For perpetual half yearly or quarterly payments, Table V. is to be applied as in similar cases of temporary annuities.

EXAMPLES.

1. What is an estate of 140 L. per annum, to continue forever, worth in present money, allowing 4 per cent. to the purchaser?

$$1.04 - 1 = .04)\overset{\text{L.}}{140.00}$$

L. 3500

2. What is the present worth of a freehold estate of 290 dollars per annum, to continue forever, allowing 4 per cent. to the purchaser? Ans. 7250 dols.

PERPETUITIES IN REVERSION.

CASE 1.

The rent of a freehold estate, time of reversion, and rate per cent. given, to find the present worth.

RULE.

Multiply the ratio involved to the time of reversion, by the ratio, less one, for a divisor; by which divide the yearly payment, the quotient will be the answer.

EXAMPLES.

1. If a freehold estate of 50 L. per annum, to commence 4 years hence, be put up at sale, what is the present worth, allowing the purchaser 5 per cent.?

Ans. 822 L. 14 s. 1 d. 2 qrs. +

Ratio involved to the time } 1.2155062
of reversion, viz., 4 years } .05 ratio less one.

.060775310)50(822 *l.* 14 *s.* 1 *d.* 2 *q.*+

2. What is an estate of 696 dols. per annum, to continue forever, but not to commence till the expiration of 4 years, worth in present money, allowance being made at 4 per cent.? Ans. 14873.594 dols.

PERMUTATION.

Permutation is a rule for finding how many different ways any given number of things may be varied in position, place, or succession; thus, a b c, a c b, b a c, b c a, c a b, c b a, are six different positions of three letters.

RULE.

Multiply all the terms of the natural series continually from one to the given number inclusive; the last product will be the answer required.

EXAMPLES.

1. In how many different positions can 6 persons place themselves at a table? $1\times2\times3\times4\times5\times6=720$. Ans.

2. How many days can 7 persons be placed in a different position at dinner? Ans. 5040 days.

3. What number of changes may be rung upon 12 bells, and in what time may they be rung, allowing 3 seconds to every change?

Ans. { 479001600 changes.
45 years, 195 days, 18 hours.

COMBINATION.

Combination is a rule for discovering how many different ways a less number of things may be combined out of a greater; thus, out of the letters a b c, are three different combinations of two; viz., ab, ac, ba.

RULE.

Take a series proceeding from and increasing by a unit, up to the number to be combined; and another series of as many places decreasing by a unit, from the number out of which the combinations are to be made; multiply the former continually for a divisor, and the latter for a dividend, the quotient will be the answer.

EXAMPLES.

1. How many combinations can be made of 5 letters out of ten.

$$\frac{10\times9\times8\times7\times6}{1\times2\times3\times4\times5}=252=\text{Ans.}$$

2. How many combinations can be made of 6 letters out of 10? Ans. 210.

3. What is the value of as many different dozens as may be chosen out of 24, at 1 d. per dozen?

Ans. 11267 L. 6 s. 4 d.

DUODECIMALS.

Duodecimals are fractions of a foot, or of an inch, or parts of an inch, &c., having 12 for their denominator.

The denominations are, foot, inch, second, third, and fourth.

12 Fourths''''	one	1 Third'''
12 Thirds	——	1 Second''
12 Seconds	——	1 Inch. *I.*
12 Inches	——	1 Foot. *Ft.*

ADDITION OF DUODECIMALS.

RULE.

Proceed as in Compound Addition.

EXAMPLES.

Ft.	*I.*	''
25	6	3
14	2	9
35	11	10
45	10	11
6	0	0
4	9	0
132	4	9

Ft.	*I.*	''
72	4	6
54	3	2
14	0	8
26	3	2
19	0	4
14	0	0

Ft.	*I.*	''	'''	''''
17	9	2	3	11
18	11	10	8	9
22	11	5	4	9
14	10	11	10	8
12	0	0	4	10
10	2	8	4	0

4. Four floors in a certain building contain each 1084 feet, 9 in. 8''; how many feet are there in all? Ans. 4339 ft. 2 in. 8''.

5. There are six mahogany boards, the first measures 27 ft. 3 in., the second, 25 ft. 11 in., the third, 23 ft. 10 in., the fourth, 20ft. 9in., the fifth, 20ft. 6in., and the sixth, 18ft. 5 in.; how many feet do they contain? Ans. 136 ft. 8 in.

SUBTRACTION OF DUODECIMALS.

RULE.

Proceed as in Compound Subtraction.

EXAMPLES.

Ft.	*I.*	''
75	9	9
14	6	11
61	2	10

Ft.	*I.*	''
84	6	4
72	9	8

Ft.	*I.*	''	'''	''''
100	10	8	10	11
97	2	4	6	8

4. If 19 ft. 10 in. be cut from a board which contains 41 ft. 7 in., how much will be left? Ans. 21 ft. 9 in.

5. Bought a raft of boards containing 59621 ft. 8 in., of which are since sold 3 parcels, each 14905 ft. 5 in.; how many feet remain? Ans. 14905 ft. 5 in.

MULTIPLICATION OF DUODECIMALS.

CASE 1.

When the feet of the multiplier do not exceed 12.

RULE.

Set the feet of the multiplier under the lowest denomination of the multiplicand, as in the following example; then multiply as in Compound Multiplication by each denomination of the multiplier separately, observing to place the right hand figure, or number, of each product, under that denomination of the multiplier by which it is produced.

Note 1.—If there are no feet in the multiplier, supply their place with a cypher; and in like manner supply the place of any other denomination between the highest and lowest.

2. Feet multiplied by feet, give feet; feet multiplied by inches, give inches; feet multiplied by seconds, give seconds; inches multiplied by inches, give seconds; inches multiplied by seconds, give thirds; seconds multiplied by seconds, give fourths.

*** It may be remarked that though the feet obtained by this rule are square feet, the inches are not square inches, but twelfth parts of a square foot.

EXAMPLES.

1. Multiply 10 ft. 6 in. by 4 ft. 6 in.

Ft.	*I.*	
10	6	
	4	6
5	3	0
42	0	
47	3	0

Or thus:

I.			
6	$\frac{1}{2}$	10	6
			4 6
		42	0
		5	3
		47	3

Or Decimally.

Ft.	*I.*	*Ft.*
10	6 =	10.5
4	6 =	4.5
		525
		420
		47.25.

	Ft.	*I.*	*″*		*Ft.*	*I.*	*″*		*Ft.*	*I.*	*″*	*‴*
2. Multiply	9	7		by	3	6		Result	33	6	6	
3. ———	3	11		by	9	5		——	36	10	7	
4. ———	8	6	9	by	7	3	8	——	62	6	7	9
5. ———	28	10	6	by	3	2	4	——	92	2	10	6

CASE 2.

When the feet of the multiplier exceed 12.

RULE.

Multiply by the feet of the multiplier, as in Compound Multiplication, and take parts for the inches, &c.

EXAMPLES.

1. Multiply 112 ft. 3 in. 5″ by 42 ft. 4 in. 6″.

		Ft.	*I.*	*″*		
		112	3	5		
				6 × 7 = 42.		
		673	8	6		
				7		
I. 4	$\frac{1}{3}$	4715	11	6	*‴*	*⁗*
		37	5	1	8	
″ 6	$\frac{1}{8}$	4	8	1	8	6
		4758	0	9	4	6

	Ft. I. ″		Ft. I. ″		Ft. I. ″ ‴
2. Multiply	76 7	by	19 10	Result	1518 10 10
3. ———	127 6	by	184 8	——	23545 0 0
4. ———	71 2 6	by	81 1 8	——	5777 9 2 2

APPLICATION.

1. A certain board is 28 ft. 10 in. 6″ long, and 3 ft. 2 in. 4″ wide; how many square feet does it contain? Ans. 92 ft. 2 in. 10″ 6‴.

2. If a board be 23 ft. 3 in. long, and 3 ft. 6 in. wide, how many square feet does it contain? Ans. 81 ft. 4 in. 6″.

3. A certain partition is 82 ft. 6 in. by 13 ft. 3 in.; how many square feet does it contain? Ans. 1093 ft. 1 in. 6″.

4. If a floor be 79 feet 8 in. by 38 ft. 11 in., how many square feet are therein? Ans. 3100 ft. 4 in. 4″.

Note.—Divide the square feet by 9, and the quotient will be square yards.

5. If a ceiling be 59 ft. 9 in. long, and 24 ft. 6 in. broad, how many square yards does it contain? Ans. 162 yd. 5 ft.+

6. What will the plastering of a ceiling come to, at 10 d. per yard, supposing the length 21 ft. 8 in., and the breadth 14 ft. 10 in.? Ans. 1 L. 9 s. 9 d.

7. What will the paving of a court-yard come to, at 4¾ d. per yard, the length being 58 feet 6 inches, and the breadth 54 feet 9 inches?

Ans. 7 L. 0 s. 10 d.

8. Suppose the dimensions of a bale to be 7 feet 6 inches, 3 feet 3 inches, and 1 foot 10 inches; what is the solid content? Ans. 44 ft. 8 in. 3′.

```
                         Ft. I.
                          7  6
                             3  3
      Ft. I.             ---------
       7  6 × 3 in. =  1 10  6
       7  6 × 3 ft. = 22  6
                       ---------
                       24  4  6
                              1 10
Ft. I. ″               ---------
24  4  6 × 10 in. = 20  3  9  0
24  4  6 ×  1 ft. = 24  4  6
                    ------------
               Ans. 44  8  3
```

9. What is the freight of a bale containing 65 feet 9 inches, at 15 dollars per ton of 40 feet? Ans. 24 dols. 65¼ cts.

```
                                          Decimally.
 | 20 ft. | 1/2  | $15.00 for 40 feet.      65.75
 |  5 ft. | 1/4  |   7.50                      15
 |  6 in. | 1/10 |   1.87.5                 -----
 |  2 in. | 1/2  |     18.7                 32875
 |        |      |      9.3                 6575
                   -------                -------
                   24.65.5              40)986.25
                                          -------
                                          24.65.6
```

10. A merchant imports from London 6 bales of the following dimensions, viz.:

	Length.		Height.		Depth.	
	Ft.	*I.*	*Ft.*	*I.*	*Ft.*	*I.*
No. 1.	2	10	2	4	1	9
2.	2	10	2	6	1	3
3.	3	6	2	2	1	8
4.	2	10	2	8	1	9
5.	2	10	2	6	1	9
6.	2	11	2	8	1	8

What are the solid contents, and how much will the freight amount to, at 20 dollars per ton?

The contents are, viz.:

No. 1.	11	7	Feet.
2.	8	10	71.58
3.	12	7	20
4.	13	2	———
5.	12	5	40)1431.60
6.	13	0	———
	———		35.79
	71	7	Amount $35.79.

PROMISCUOUS QUESTIONS.

1. A merchant had 1000 dollars in bank; he drew out at one time $237.50, at another time $116.09, and at another $241.06¼; after which he deposited at one time 1500 dollars, and at another time $750.50; how much had he in bank after making the last deposit? Ans. $2655.84¼.

2. Sold 8 bales of linen, 4 of which contained 9 pieces each, and in each piece was 35 yards; the other 4 bales contained 12 pieces each, and in each piece was 27 yards: how many pieces and how many yards were in all? Ans. 84 pieces, 2556 yards.

3. A was born when B was 21 years of age, how old will A be when B is 47; and what will be the age of B when A is 60?

Ans. { A will be 26 when B is 47.
B will be 81 when A is 60.

4. If 79 L. 4 s. 10 d. be divided among 4 men, 6 women, and 9 boys, so as that each man shall receive twice as much as a woman, and each woman twice as much as a boy, what will be the share of each?

Ans. { Each boy must have 2 L. 2 s. 10 d.
Each woman - - 4 L. 5 s. 8d.
Each man - - 8 L. 11 s. 4d.

5. How many bushels of wheat, at $1.12 per bushel, can I have for $81.76? Ans. 73.

6. What will 27 cwt. of iron come to, at $4.56 per cwt.? Ans. $123.12.

7. When a man's yearly income is 949 dollars, how much is it per day? Ans. $2.60.

8. If a man leave 6509 dollars to his wife and two sons thus—to his wife ⅓,

to his elder son 3-5 of the remainder, and to his other son the rest; what is the share of each?

Ans. { Wife's share $2440.87½. Elder son's $2440.87½. Other son's $1627.25.

9. How many yards of cloth, at 17 s. 6 d. per yard, can I have for 13 cwt. 2 qrs. of wool, at 14 d. per lb.? Ans. 100 yards 3 1-5 qrs.

10. How many dollars are equal to 980 French crowns? Ans. 1078.

11. If goods which cost 10 s. be sold for 11 s. 9 d., what is the gain per cent.? Ans. 17½.

12. Bought 27 bags of ginger, each weighing gross 84¾ lb., tare 1¼ lb. per bag, tret 4 lb. per 104 lb.; what does the whole (neat weight) come to, at 8½ d. per lb.? Ans. 76 L. 13 s. 2¾ d.

13. My factor sends me word he has bought goods to the value of 500 L. 13 s. 6 d. upon my account; what will his commission come to at 3½ per cent.? Ans. 17 L. 10 s. 5¼ d.

14. If ⅜ of an ounce cost ⅞ of a shilling, what will 5-6 of a lb. cost? Ans. 17 s. 6 d.

15. If 5-6 of a gallon cost ⅜ of a L., what will 5-9 of a tun cost? Ans. 105 L.

16. If ⅜ of a ship be worth 3740 L., what is the worth of the whole? Ans. 9973 L. 6 s. 8 d.

17. A person who was possessed of 2-5 of a vessel, sold ⅝ of his share for 375 L.; what was the whole vessel worth at that rate? Ans. 1500 L.

18. If 4½ cwt. be carried 36 miles for 35 s., how many pounds can I have carried 20 miles for the same money? Ans. 907 lb. 3 oz. 3 dr. 4-20.

19. What is the interest of 47 L. 10 s. for 4 years and 52 days, at 4¼ per cent.? Ans. 8 L. 17 s. 1 d.

20. If 100 L. in 5 years gain 20 L. 10 s., in what time will any sum of money double itself at the same rate of interest? Ans. 24 16-41 years.

21. What sum will produce as much interest in 3½ years, as 210 L. 3s. would in 5 years and 5 months? Ans. 350 L. 5 s.

22. What is the commission on $2176.50 at 2½ per cent.? Ans. $54.41 1-5.

23. What is the premium of insuring 1650 dollars, at 15½ per cent.? Ans. $255.75.

24. Bought a quantity of goods for 250 L., and 3 months afterwards sold them for 275 L.; how much per cent. per annum was gained by the transaction? Ans. 40 L.

25. A vintner mixed 20 gallons of port wine, at 5 s. 4 d. per gallon, with 12 gallons of white wine, at 5 s. per gallon, 30 gallons of Lisbon, at 6 s. per gallon, and 20 gallons of mountain, at 4 s. 6 d. per gallon; what was a gallon of the mixture worth? Ans. 5 s. 3¾ d. +

26. A person has two silver cups of unequal weight, having one cover to both, which weighs 5 oz.; now if the cover be put on the less cup, it will be double the weight of the greater cup, and put on the greater cup, it will be three times as heavy as the less cup; what is the weight of each cup? Ans. The less 3 oz. the greater 4 oz.

27. A person said he had 20 children, and that it happened there was a year and a half between each of their ages; his eldest son was born when he was 24 years old, and the age of his youngest is 21; what was the father's age? Ans. 73½ years.

28. In a certain orchard ½ of the trees bear apples, ¼ pears, 1-6 plums, 60 of them peaches, and 40 cherries; how many trees are in the orchard? Ans. 1200.

29. If by selling goods at 50 s. per cwt. I gain 20 per cent., what do I gain or lose per cent. by selling at 45 s. per cwt.? Ans. 8 L. gain.

30. Sold goods for 63 L., and by so doing lost 17 per cent., whereas I ought, in dealing, to have cleared 20 per cent.; how much under their just value were they sold? Ans. 28 L. 1 s. 8 d.

31. A person willing to distribute some money among a number of beggars, wanted 8 d. to give them 3 d. a piece; he therefore gave each 2 d. and had 3 d. left; how many beggars were there? Ans. 11.

32. A person being asked the hour of the day, said: "The time past noon is equal to 4-5 of the time till midnight;" what was the time? Ans. 20 minutes past 5.

33. A person looking on his watch, was asked what was the time of day, who answered, "It is between 4 and 5;" but a more particular answer being required, he said that the hour and minute hands were then exactly together; what was the time? Ans. 21 9-11 minutes past 4.

34. Two men depart from the same place at the same time; one travels 30 and the other 35 miles a day; how far are they distant from each other after 7 days, supposing them both to travel the same road; and how far, if they travel in contrary directions?

Ans. { 35 miles, when going the same way, 455 miles, ——— contrary ways.

35. A guardian paid his ward 3500 L. for 2500 L. which he had held in possession 8 years; what rate of interest did he allow him? Ans. 5 per cent.

36. In what time will any sum of money double itself, at 6 per cent. interest? Ans. 16 years and 8 months.

37. A owes B 100 L., payable in 3½ months, 150 L. in 4½ months, and 204 L. in 5¾ months, and is willing to make one payment of the whole; in what time should the payment be made? Ans. 4 months 23 days +

38. If the earth be 360 degrees in circumference, and each degree 69½ miles, how long would a man be in travelling round it, who advances 20 miles a day; reckoning 365¼ days in a year? Ans. 3 years 155¼ days.

39. A minor of 14 had an annuity left him of 400 dollars a year, the proceeds of which, by will, was to be put out, both principal and interest, yearly as it fell due, at 5 per cent., until he should arrive at 21 years of age; what had he then to receive? Ans. $3256.80 +

40. If a piece of marble be 47 inches long, 47 inches broad, and 47 inches deep, how many cubical inches does it contain? Ans. 103823.

41. There is a cellar dug that is 12 feet every way, in length, breadth, and depth; how many solid feet of earth were taken out of it? Ans. 1728.

42. How many bricks, 9 inches long and 4 inches wide, will pave a yard that is 20 feet square? Ans. 1600.

43. If A can do a piece of work alone in 7 days, and B in 12 days, in what time can they finish it, both working together? Ans. 4 8-19 days.

44. A and B traded together; A put in 320 L. for 5 months, B 460 L. for 3 months, and they gained 100 L.; what is each man's share of the gain?

Ans. { A's share is 53 L. 13 s. 9 d. + B's share is 46 L. 6 s. 2 d. +

45. What is the value of a slab of marble, the length of which is 5 feet 7 inches, and the breadth 1 foot 10 inches, at 1 dollar per foot? Ans. $10.23¼.

46. A certain stone measures 4 feet 6 inches in length, 2 feet 9 inches in breadth, and 3 feet 4 inches in depth; how many solid feet does it contain?

Ans. 41 feet 3 inches.

47. Shipped to Jamaica 550 pair of stockings, at 11s. 6d. per pair, and 460 yards of stuff, at 14 d. per yard; in return for which I have received 40 cwt. 3 qrs. of sugar, at 24 s. 6 d. per cwt., and 1570 lb. of indigo, at 2 s. 4 d. per lb.; what remains due to me? Ans. 102 L. 12 s. 11¼ d.

48. If the flash of an ordnance was observed just one minute and three seconds before the report, what was the distance; supposing the flash to be seen the instant of its going off, and admitting the sound to fly at the rate of 1142 feet in a second? Ans. 13 miles 5 fur. +

49. Which would be preferable, an annual rent of 876 dollars clear, for 12 years, to be received in quarterly payments, or 7200 dollars in hand, reckoning interest at 5 per cent.? Ans. The annuity by 1272 dols. +

50. A line 35 yards long will exactly reach from the top of a fort, standing on the brink of a river, to the opposite bank, known to be 27 yards from the foot of the wall; what is the height of the wall? Ans. 22 yds. 9¾ in. +

51. Bought 120 apples at 2 for a penny, and 120 more at 3 for a penny, and sold them altogether at 5 for 2d.; what did I gain or lose by the bargain?

Ans. Lost 4 d.

52. A cistern for water has 2 cocks to supply it, by the first it may be filled in 45 minutes, and by the second in 55 minutes; it has likewise a discharging cock, by which it may, when full, be emptied in 30 minutes; now if these three cocks be all left open when the water comes in, in what time will the cistern be filled? Ans. 2 hours, 21 min. 25 5-7 sec.

53. The account of a certain school is as follows, viz.: 1-16 of the boys learn geometry, ⅜ learn grammar, 3-10 learn arithmetic, 3-20 learn to write, and 9 learn to read; what number is there of each?

Ans. { 5 who learn geometry, 30 grammar, 24 arithmetic, 12 writing, and 9 reading.

54. The sales of certain goods amount to $1873.40; what sum is to be received for them, allowing 2½ per cent. for commission, and ¼ per cent. for prompt payment of the neat proceeds? Ans. $1821.99¾ +

www.ingramcontent.com/pod-product-compliance
Lightning Source LLC
LaVergne TN
LVHW011224110826
845150LV00006B/1537
9781425515799